VIGNETTES FROM VIETNAM

BRIEF MOMENTS OF SANITY

And Belated Notes of Gratitude

VIGNETTES FROM
VIETNAM

BRIEF MOMENTS OF SANITY

And Belated Notes of Gratitude

BRICE H. BARNES

DENVER, COLORADO

Vignettes From Vietnam
Brief Moments of Sanity
And Belated Notes of Gratitude
All Rights Reserved.
Copyright © 2014 Brice H. Barnes
v2.0 r1.0

Outskirts Press, Inc.
http://www.outskirtspress.com

ISBN: 978-1-4787-3013-2

Outskirts Press and the "OP" logo are trademarks belonging to Outskirts Press, Inc.

Table of Contents

Foreword

THE 9TH INFANTRY Division was unique in that the division was first formed at Fort Riley, Kansas, under the leaders who would take the troops into combat. Once the ranks were filled, these leaders took the soldiers first through basic, then advanced individual, then unit training. The 2nd Battalion (Mechanized), 47th Infantry, which was a part of the 9th Division, arrived in Vietnam by ship in January, 1967 as a tight-knit, fully trained outfit led by the officers and NCOs who had trained it. Unfortunately, a program known as "infusion" began to break up the closeness the 9th Division soldiers had carried with them from Fort Riley. Infusion was designed to keep the entire division from rotating home at the same time after a year's tour. Soldiers with different departure dates were transferred in and some of the old Fort Riley crowd were transferred out. In addition, casualties had to be replaced.

Brice Barnes and I were two of several replacement officers who were assigned to the battalion about six months after they arrived in country. I was assigned to C Company, and Brice went to B Company. It is common for non-Texans to believe that all things from Texas are large. Brice Barnes is the exception to that belief. In Vietnam, he stood about 5'6' and probably weighed less than 130 pounds, at least a pound of which was made up of moustache. What he lacked in stature, he made up for with charisma, personality, bravado, leadership ability, and pure Texas B.S.

Naturally, the Fort Riley officers assumed they would continue in key leadership positions and would be selected for company command when those positions opened up. Many were disappointed and resentful when newly arrived replacements took coveted assignments. Captain Bill Tomlinson, a replacement officer, a lawyer by training and a renegade infantryman by choice, was given command of B Company over some of the Fort Riley officers. Brice Barnes took one of Tomlinson's platoons. I served as a platoon leader and executive officer, and eventually company commander in C Company. As replacement outsiders, Brice and I became fast friends. Resentment by the original veterans festered and quickly hampered the morale of the battalion. Soon, however, the combination of new leaders' personalities and styles sparked B Company to become a rowdy, happy-go-lucky outfit. In the autumn of 1967, Barnes' platoon discovered what would turn out to be the largest enemy weapons cache of the entire Vietnam War. Bill Tomlinson would go on to be awarded the Distinguished Service Cross, second only to the Medal of Honor as a combat decoration, during a battle immediately preceding the Tet Offensive.

Barnes would later take over the battalion's reconnaissance (Scout) platoon which was suffering from poor morale, mostly caused by their outgoing platoon leader. When Barnes arrived in the platoon, their morale instantly shot through the roof. His participating style of leadership, his willingness to do anything he required his troops to do, his sense of humor, and his desire to take care of his subordinates, no matter what the situation, instantly endeared him to his soldiers.

On 31 January 1968, Brice Barnes led his Scout Platoon in a successful counter attack against a Viet Cong/NVA battalion which was poised to initiate an attack against the U.S. II Field Force Headquarters in *Long Binh*. The Viet Cong and North Vietnamese forces had used a village that housed the dependents of deceased South Vietnamese soldiers as an attack position. The Scouts stopped their attack cold. In the day-long battle that ensued, the small Scout Platoon, eventually reinforced by a rifle company, destroyed an entire Viet Cong battalion, suffering only one soldier killed by the enemy, but another fatality caused by our Military Police. Several Scouts were wounded in this battle. Once Widows' Village, as it was known, was cleared, Barnes and his platoon were ordered to come to the aid of C Company, which I commanded, fighting its way through the village of *Ho Nai*. C Company was attacking eastward through the village and the Scout Platoon attacked westward, trapping another Viet Cong battalion between us. Barnes' Scouts were ambushed and an hours-long fight followed. With one of its armored personnel carriers destroyed and one soldier killed and many wounded, Barnes and his men fought their way out. For his actions on this day, he was awarded the Distinguished Service Cross.

Brice Barnes exemplifies the example of the citizen soldier. He first joined the Texas National Guard a few years out of high school. His test scores and his demonstrated leadership ability marked him as a candidate for becoming an officer. After completing Officers' Candidate School and the Infantry Officers' Basic Course at Fort Benning, Georgia, he was assigned to active duty. He served a short stint in the 1st Armored Division, and then was assigned to Vietnam. It must be pointed out that Barnes, with less than a full college education, held his own, and even excelled when competing with ROTC and West Point officers.

After Vietnam, Barnes was initially assigned to the 4th Army at Ft. Sam Houston, Texas as a contingency plans officer. Upon the recommendation of his commanding general, he was accepted into the degree completion program and in1970, graduated from the University of Texas at Austin with a BA degree in government. After receiving his degree, he was once again assigned to Vietnam, this time with the 199th Light Infantry Brigade. There he served as a rifle company commander and logistics officer. When the 199th redeployed to the U.S., Barnes finished his tour as an advisor to the Vietnamese, then was assigned to Thailand.

Returning to the states, Barnes left the active army and was again assigned to the Texas National Guard as an educated, decorated combat officer. He rose rapidly in rank, serving in both the guard and reserves, ultimately serving in a brigade-equivalent capacity. He furthered his education in the Armor Officers' Advanced Course, Command and General Staff College and the Tactical Commanders' Development Course at Fort Leavenworth, Kansas.

Brice Barnes retired as a full colonel in 1993, completing thirty years as the consummate citizen soldier. Since retiring, he has remained in service, actively supporting the 47th Infantry Association. In 2010, he was selected as the Honorary Colonel of the 47th Infantry Regiment. During his watch, the association has completed two extremely successful reunions and the dedication of the 47th Regiment monument at Fort Benning. Largely due to his personal efforts, many Vietnam Veterans from the Regiment were added to the roles of the Association, and reunited with many Brothers at subsequent Reunions. He has also crusaded to have the Valorous Unit Award given to the 2nd Battalion (Mechanized), 47th Infantry for its actions during the Tet Offensive, upgraded to the Presidential Unit Citation it deserves.

During a raucous evening at the 2010 reunion of the 47th Regiment, a group of old veterans sat around singing our old songs. Brice looked at me and asked, "Do you remember our song?" Without further ado, we burst into Shell Silversteen's *"After You've Been Eating Steak a Long Time, Beans Taste Fine"*. We had last sung this song at the battalion's officers' club in 1968. At the reunion, we sang it as if we had been rehearsing for a month. Some memories never die.

John E. Gross,
Lieutenant Colonel, US Army (Retired), Infantry

Preface

BEFORE LEAVING THE States for my second tour in the Republic of Vietnam, I visited with the Managing Editor of the *Austin American-Statesman* to inquire if he would be interested in receiving first-hand, eye-witness reports from Vietnam. I explained that I was returning for my second tour, and would send them periodic articles about what I had seen and learned, and if suitable, printable in the paper. They agreed to my proposal, and would pay the princely sum of $10 for every article published, with checks going to my parents, since I had no way of cashing them in Vietnam. This was the origin of my writing career, spotted and intermittent as it is. After these series of articles, my writing efforts were basically dormant until the late 80's.

In 1988, I was participating in a Vietnam Veterans discussion group when the leader asked each of us to write a story, article, letter or whatever form we wanted about the most traumatic and important event that occurred to us while in Vietnam. For me, the choice was obvious, namely my participation in the Tet Counter-Offensive of 1968. In order to write this story, I consulted the various notes, charts and diagrams that I had created shortly after the various battles of that day in which the 2nd Battalion 47th Infantry (Mechanized) participated, in anticipation of writing an article for the *Infantry* magazine, thinking that what my Scout Platoon had accomplished should be the new Field Manual for Mechanized Infantry! But fortunately, reality and other important events quickly overruled my gigantic ego, and I stuck my notes etc. back into that folder to await a better time and audience. And hopefully, a healthy dose of modesty. Within two weeks after I finished writing about the Battle of Widows' Village and other actions during Tet, I received a hand-written envelope from the Department of the Army, and inside it was a typewritten letter from Keith W. Nolan, a noted military historian. Nolan was requesting the recipient to be interviewed about a book that he wanted to write about the history of the Tet Offensive as it related to Saigon and its environs. There were copies of reviews about other books that Nolan had written, and he seemed to be favorably accepted by Veterans and Active Duty folks alike. After a couple of telephone conversations with Keith, I volunteered to mail him a copy of what I had just written, and invited him to use any or none of it in the preparation of his book. Several months later, Keith sent me the galley proofs of his *The Battle for Saigon: Tet 1968*, and asked me to critique it, especially Chapter 14, which dealt with the Battle of Widows' Village. There were only a few minor editorial corrections that I could offer Keith, and did so before mailing the galley proofs back to him. Keith and I communicated sporadically after that, and it was only later that I learned of his untimely death at a very young age. We Vietnam Veterans lost a true friend and advocate that day. I have a personally autographed copy of one of his books, one of my most prized possessions. After my "contribution" to his book, that was the end of my writing career until I received an electronic copy of a proposed article for the *Vietnam* magazine that a fellow Vietnam Veteran had written, also about the Battle for

Widows' Village. From my perspective, that article was so full of factual errors, tactical impossibilities, and physical improbabilities that I wrote a strongly worded reply, after first checking with my former Scouts who had witnessed and participated in the Battle. In commenting on my rebuttal to his proposed article, I was encouraged by my Scouts to do more writing, a suggestion that went into the "Latent Idea File."

In 2008, I was offered a part-time position with the Northrop Grumman Corporation, which had a contract with the US Army, to do essentially what I was doing with the Army before I retired. And as you can guess, with any government related work effort, there is a substantial amount of 'downtime,' non-productive breaks, and hours after work, with no household chores! During one of these periods of slack time, I remarked to one of my fellow workers about an incident that reminded me of the story about some venison sausage I had received in a "goodie" package from my father during my first tour in Vietnam. After I told him my story, he related that I ought to write it down, as somebody else might enjoy it as well. And so the writing effort began anew! As I was reminded of certain events that had occurred, another vignette was added to the growing number of stories. Just for critical feedback, I had sent copies of various vignettes to different folks, and basically incorporated all relevant comments and criticisms as appropriate in the edited version. It also became apparent to me that I had not properly expressed my gratitude to all the great warriors, friends, family members, and to God Himself for all the blessings the aforementioned have provided, and are continuing to provide in my life. You gentle readers will note that at the end of each vignette, I thank the appropriate person for the lesson learned, gift received, or blessing acknowledged. It's the very least I can do now, and being reminded to be more grateful in the future, starting on a daily basis!

Naturally, I want to express my profound gratitude to my literary mentor, great friend, and fellow raconteur, John E. Gross. John's excellent book, an autobiographical novel, *Jupiter 6*, not only entertained me, but inspired me to undertake my own writing project, albeit on a much more modest scale. John is one of those unforgettable characters who inspired his men to perform at several levels above their imagined or real capabilities, leading them with consummate skills, charm, and charisma that he used in all other assignments and activities. He is still held in a position of awed reverence by his men, for very good reason. To those others mentioned in the various tales are also owed a special debt of gratitude, for without their magnificent contributions to my safety, sanity and whatever successes I have enjoyed, none of this written effort would have happened.

I also wish to express my appreciation to the publishers and managers of the *Austin American-Statesman* for their kind permission to reprint the articles I wrote during my second tour in Vietnam, articles that were ultimately printed in the local newspaper. Those articles provided another springboard to subsequent writing efforts, which have now culminated in this book. The publishers of *Vietnam* magazine are also due special thanks for printing an edited version of my story about the Battle of Widows' Village in their February 2014 issue of their stellar magazine. The unedited story is included in this little tome of mine.

But the greatest debt of gratitude I have is to those men and women I had the honor of commanding in battle and in peacetime, and to those fellow officers, non-commissioned officers, and enlisted men and women that I served with in the Active Army, in the Texas Army National Guard and in the Army Reserve. My military travels – besides Vietnam, Cambodia, Thailand, Japan, Malaysia and Taiwan – have included repeated stays at Fort Hood, Texas, Fort Knox, Kentucky, for some armor schooling, Fort Leavenworth, Kansas for some advanced leader schooling, Fort Benning, Georgia for various Infantry courses, and various Army Reserve posts. In each place, I encountered men and women, who for the most part, were dedicated soldiers, doing the jobs for which they enlisted or commissioned, proudly serving our great country. Together, these people taught me many lessons of life, probably saved my life because of their actions, and ultimately helped me to become a better person. While I cannot name them all personally, their cumulative imprint on my life is something for which I'll be forever grateful. Thank You, one and all, for being in my life.

Introduction

TOO MUCH HAS been written, filmed and otherwise communicated about the War in Vietnam that is negative, vulgar, obscene, insulting, and generally worthless from an instructive, informational, or cultural point of view. For example, we were regaled with a movie in which the average Grunt was portrayed as nothing more than a dope-smoking, village burning, woman raping, baby-killer. After exiting the theater from viewing this cinematic piece of trash, I was forced to steady my nerves with a double-shot of good Scotch whiskey. Just thinking about this movie almost makes me want to go back to serious drinking again! I resolved then and there to be more discerning about the movies or television shows I would view in the future. I also promised myself that I would never watch another production by Oliver Stone. We were told by another Vietnam Veteran that war crimes had been frequently committed, even observed by the author of that statement in a committee hearing before U. S. Congress. We also learned that he failed to stop or even report such atrocities to the proper authorities, as he was charged to do by both his oath of office and by the Laws of the Geneva Convention. His fellow travelers and Communist sympathizers in this anti-military/anti-war charade later confessed that they had not even been to Vietnam, much less served as an observer of the heinous acts as reported by their leader, now the Secretary of State, John Kerry. But the imagery as described by Kerry and other charlatans has stuck in the American psyche, and only recently have the lies been exposed to the absolute light of truth, and healing has subsequently begun. Many of us will probably go to our graves before any apology or request for forgiveness is uttered by John Kerry. Like most charlatans, his apology will ring hollow. Because he dishonored so many of us, the near-universal disdain for him is palpable. For years, many of us were ashamed to be known as a Vietnam Veteran, but now, being a Vietnam Veteran is an honorable thing indeed. The growing list of "wannabees," those lower forms of human life that pretend to be Vietnam Veterans, simply proves that we are now acceptable in American society. For those of us who have silently borne our past, we are now proudly emerging from the shadows, to claim our rightful place in American history.

I have also read that even one of our former Panthers and his brother have made some broad-brush indictments of the officers, NCO's and other enlisted men of the 2nd Battalion, 47th Infantry, during our time in Vietnam. Their comments were posted on some Internet website for the entire world to see and read, much to the consternation and disgust of those who served honorably with this Army unit. The officers were called incompetent, the NCO's drunks, and the enlisted men nothing more than dope heads. One has to wonder how these sterling examples of self-promotion managed to survive their tour in Vietnam, surrounded by all this incompetence, drunkenness, and aromatic smoke. And now one of these brothers serves as the Secretary of Defense. God help our current warriors. With "friends" like the Hagel's, I'm compelled all the more to make my voice heard in an attempt to set the record straight in the face of these slanderous lies. Since I continue to hold my men in such high regard, dishonoring the men I had the honor of leading is an unforgiveable sin, in my humble opinion. I will take whatever opportunity that presents itself to defend and honor my fellow warriors.

Admittedly, I cannot refute every critic of the war in Vietnam, nor will I defend those who may have committed a war crime. That is not the purpose of this book. What I am trying to do is to convey is a more balanced paradigm of the war in Vietnam in its entirety, especially from a Grunt's viewpoint. Most of us didn't hate the Vietnamese, just those trying to kill us. Their values, even the most dedicated Viet Cong, were basically the same as what we embraced and endorsed, an appreciation for life, a love of family, and commitment to a cause greater than ourselves. Unfortunately, our current warriors have had to fight against the most ignoble savagery of Islamic fundamentalism whose value system is diametrically opposed to everything we hold dear. The battles which our current warriors fight are a much more difficult war than ours was, and I hold them in utmost respect and admiration. As I recently remarked to a young warrior fresh from another deployment to Afghanistan, "I still retain the skill-sets I used most effectively some 40+ years ago, but prefer not to have to use them today, so Thank You for protecting us old gray-beards!" I will always maintain that our very reason for being in Vietnam was a noble cause indeed, trying to prevent yet another country from falling under the crushing boot of Communist tyranny and brutality. Just as history has a way of repeating itself, the war we won militarily in Vietnam bears mind-numbing similarities to the successful war in Iraq, where politicians have surrendered the victories for political expediency. Pulling certain defeat out of the jaws of victory is a phrase that comes to mind. Perhaps the greatest irony of the entire war in Vietnam is that the country, now recognized as one, operates outwardly as a communistic economy, yet the "underground economy" is distinctively capitalistic in nature and result. We can only pray that freedom will ultimately reign supreme there. That hope goes double for freedom of religion.

I confess that my little stories are only a microcosmic view of what was happening in Vietnam, sans any political imprints or attitudes about the correctness about our involvement there. My purpose in this writing is to convey a bit of humanity into what sometimes were inhuman circumstances, to add some personal touches, and to offer anything that I can to aid in the healing of old wounds. As the title also suggests, I want to extend some long over-due thanks to certain individuals whose contributions to the vignettes made this entire book possible.

Dedication

IN 2010, I was selected to be the Honorary Colonel of the 47th Infantry Regiment, succeeding many fine officers who had held that title, and an honor that has held many challenges, but many more rewards. It was my mission and firm resolve to help the Regimental Association grow into the dynamic organization that it is today. During my tenure, and even before, I started doing some research to find out more about the history of the Regiment, and learned how famous the 47th truly is! The regimental crest tells much of the history of the unit that is one of the most highly decorated infantry regiments in the entire United States Army. From the imperial Chinese dragon, which tells of the regimental precedents in China during the Boxer Rebellion, to the crossed ivy in the center of the Crest, symbolizing the Regiment's assignment to the 4th Infantry Division, the Regiment has readily adapted to the changing military vicissitudes, always ready to serve this great nation in whatever task that has been assigned. As part of the 4th Infantry Division during World War I, the Regiment acquitted itself heroically in the battles of the Meuse-Argonne forest, at St. Mihiel, and other battle locales. After the First World War, the Regiment was reassigned to the 9th Infantry Division in 1940, and began preparations to enter World War II. Fighting from northern African to Sicily and then to Normandy, the Regiment was the first Allied unit to cross the Rhine River into Nazi Germany at the Remagen Bridge. And finally, in the run-up of the war in Vietnam, the 9th Infantry Division was re-organized, with the 47th Infantry Regiment being an integral part of that effort in Southeast Asia. Now with a total of 25 Campaign Streamers, (seven) 7 Presidential Unit Citations, (three) 3 Valorous Unit Awards, and (eight) 8 foreign Citations of Honor and Gallantry, the 47th Infantry Regiment is one of the most highly decorated units in the entire U.S. Army.

The long list of honors and awards that have been bestowed upon the Regiment only attest to the sterling contributions it has made, and continues to make in defense of our nation's liberties and freedoms. And so the Regiment – at least the 2nd Battalion - carries on the finest tradition it first established in 1900, training the latest group of warriors to stand in the breach and to guard the ramparts, wherever called to do so. So it is to this Regiment, and to its warriors, past, present and future, that I dedicate this book, with my abiding prayers of strength, commitment and resolve being imparted to all. I was truly honored to be a small part of it during the tumultuous times of the Vietnam War, and continued to do so in my current capacity as Honorary Colonel of the Regiment.

Trading C-Rations for Bullets

AFTER COMPLETING THE in-country training offered by the "Old Reliable Academy" at Camp Bearcat, I was assigned to the 2nd Battalion (Mechanized), 47th Infantry. This assignment, in and of itself, was a stroke of luck, karma, or being in the right place at the right time. Or maybe it was caused by something, someone, at a much higher level. Initially, I was selected – or condemned, depending on one's perspective – to go to the Mekong Delta for assignment with the 3rd Battalion, 39th Infantry, but in a meeting with the Division G-1 or Personnel Office, another brand new in-country officer, 2LT Dave Williams, the designated assignee to the 2-47th Infantry (Mechanized), complained to the G-1. "Sir, Barnes here just came from a mechanized unit in the States, and I don't know anything about tracks. Can we trade?" So Williams became a mud-duck in the Delta, and I was destined to a slightly faster pace of war. Mechanized. Sadly I must report, Lieutenant David William's name is now engraved on The Wall. Belated, I wrote a poetic tribute to him which is now included on his memorial page on the Internet.

Unceremoniously deposited at the front door of the S-1, 2-47th Infantry (Mechanized), Captain Greenfield told me to take all my belongings to Company B's officers' hootch, and then report back to him. "Bring all your field gear, and report back here at 1400 hours, as you're going out to the field to meet the Old Man." The Old Man in this case was LTC Arthur Moreland, a laidback and easy going commander, who would later become my mentor and protector. As it turned out, my first exposure to the Battalion was with the Scout Platoon, riding with "Moose" Bartol, as the Platoon was given the mission of providing security while the Battalion Surgeon and other medical personnel performed a MEDCAP, a Medical Civic Action Program in a nearby village. In addition to practicing some good old fashioned altruism, the MEDCAP's were also an opportunity to do a little intelligence gathering without arousing too much suspicion. How many fighting-age men were in the hamlet compared to the number of 'houses'? If there were 20 houses in the hamlet, and only 2 fighting-age men there, where were the other 18? Were they out in the rice paddies working? Were they at other jobs? Could all of them be accounted for, or were some off in the nearby woods, up to some nefarious activity? How were the local folks reacting to the Americans? What special needs might they have that if provided, might make them more pro-American and pro-South Vietnamese government?

While all this intelligence stuff was happening, I was being introduced to *Co Anh*, the nominal leader of the children in the hamlet. Despite the shouts of *di di mau* – 'beat it!' or 'scram,' in American lingo - by some of the other GI's who didn't want the children around them, *Co Anh* was very persistent, at least at Bartol's track. Earlier, I had looked up some words in my "Vietnamese-English" dictionary, and learned that "*Co*" was the word for young lady. She and the others had gathered about Bartol's armored personnel carrier and began the time-honored practice of trying to mooch food from the G.I.'s. Somehow along the way, *Co Anh*, whom I guessed to be about 12 years old, had learned a smattering of English, however grammatically incorrect it may have been. "What you name? What that?"

she asked, pointing to my 2LT bar on my collar. Quickly looking up that answer in my "Vietnamese-English" dictionary, a
pre-deployment gift from my very good friend, Dwight Davis,
I replied, "*Tu Oui* Barnes." "*Tu Oui* Bahns," she repeated, "you
give me chop-chop!" The bargaining had begun.

But being of good Scottish blood, I couldn't just give
away the bounty of my country, even if at the time it was
represented by various cans of C-rations. "OK, you bring me
bullets," I said, holding up an example, "and I give you chop-
chop." It seems that I could match her pigeon-English quite
well, complete with grammatical incorrectness. With this bit
of international negotiations out of the way, the crowd of children disappeared for good, I thought; either my bargaining
skills were lacking, or I scared them away with the offer, or
they were going to seek a better deal with another American
somewhere else. Less than 20 minutes later, they started coming back to Bartol's track, bringing everything from a single
bullet to a partial belt of M-60 machinegun ammunition, to
a 40mm "Duster" round. But *Co Anh* was wise beyond her
years. She had learned that some C-ration cans have a distinct
rattle when shook – the tasteless white bread, for instance.
"Numbah 10!" and then the can came sailing back into
Bartol's track. She wanted something better than the white
bread, and I couldn't blame her. In all I procured two sandbags full of various rounds of ammunition, with the thought
that every one that I traded for was one less that could be fired
at my men or me. Total cost to Uncle Sam: less than two cases
of C-rations. Greater peace of mind for me: Priceless!

When we returned to the Battalion' 'laager' position,
I turned in my two sandbags full of bartered ammo over to
the S-4, thinking that I was going to have to pay for giving
2 cases of C-rations away. After I asked him what I owed
the Government, the Supply Sergeant just stared at me in

disbelief, muttering something about 'dumb butter-bars' as he walked away. So much for the ballyhooed program of "Supply Economy" that they taught us about in the States!

Several months later, while in our tactical road march, I had the opportunity to stop right across Highway 15 from *Co Anh's* house. She came running across the open field, and when she saw me, she shouted, "*Tu Oui* Bahns, *Tu Oui* Bahns!" I was duly impressed that she had remembered my name! But by this time, I had been promoted to first lieutenant, or *Trung Oui*. I flipped my flak jacket open and showed her my silver bar, and re-introduced myself as "*Trung Oui* Bahns!" And this time, *Co Anh* wasn't mooching chop-chop, but wanted some soap. As it turned out, she learned from that MEDCAP of several months ago that soap was a proper remedy for *impetigo*, a common skin disease or condition most readily treated by soap and clean water. Her little brother, she explained, was a victim. I could provide some soap, but could do nothing about the cleanliness of the water. And I knew that soap was a big resale item on the black market, even in *Co Anh's* little hamlet.

Reaching into an open SP pack, I pulled out two bars of soap, and little *Co Anh's* eyes lit up in anticipation! But being practical, I cut one of the bars in half with my machete, and told here, "This is for your little brother." She glared her anger and disappointment at my generosity, until I handed her the uncut bar, and said, "And this one is for *Co Anh*!" knowing full well that she would soon sell it. The sparkle quickly returned to her eyes. I hope she made a great profit. It was the least I could do for her. And I hope she survived that terrible war, and possibly came to America. Thank you, 'Moose' Bartol, for introducing me to the Scouts, a unit I would later lead, and Thank You, Dwight Davis, for that very useful Vietnamese Phrase Book. Finally, Thank You, *Co Anh*, for teaching me a little bit of humility and humanity. I hope you were able to find your way to freedom.

My Introduction to Dionne Warwick

PREPARING FOR ANOTHER operation in an area southeast of our base camp at Camp Bearcat always caused a flurry of activities, and these actions involved dozens of people. Commanders had been briefed and were finishing preparing their maps, junior leaders were supervising the loading of the armored personnel carriers, or 'tracks,' as we called them the NCO's were getting all the troop's gear ready to be loaded on the tracks, medics were re-inventorying their aid bags for the umpteenth time, and ammunition was replenished in the ammo boxes onboard each track. The mechanics and mainte- nance crews were finishing their pre-movement maintenance checklists, and topping off the vehicles with fuel.

On cue, all the men started bringing their personal gear and weapons to be loaded on the tracks, vacating their hootches for the foreseeable future. Most men carried their own duffel bag, webgear and weapon to the tracks, and proper loading was accomplished under the supervision of the NCO's. And then there was Novello, my platoon medic. Normally, I would expect to see Specialist 5 Bruce Novello carrying his aid bag and personal gear, but instead he had what appeared to be a Samsonite suitcase in this right hand and a stack of LP's stuck up under his left arm. (Remember, this was back in the 60's, long before the invention of MP3's and other techno-toys!) As it turned out, he had already loaded his aid bag, weapon and other personal gear on an earlier trip from his hootch. But a suitcase? When I asked him why he was bringing a suitcase, he replied, "It's not a suitcase, it's a record player." Well now, that made perfectly good sense! Of course, every mechanized infantry platoon goes to war with a record player, right? Well, apparently Bravo 3-6 and his men were doing just that! I was still in a learning mode as the new second lieutenant!

The trip to our new area of operations was uneventful, and we arrived at our initial company position with about an hour of daylight remaining. Immediately after positioning the three tracks of my platoon in our assigned sector of the company perimeter, the men set about doing their regular chores of emplacing Claymore mines, setting trip flares, determining aiming points and assigning sectors of fire for the machine guns, while the drivers performed post-operations maintenance on our very old and tired tracks. Others were busy constructing fighting positions between the tracks, filling sand bags, stringing commo wire to connect all fighting positions with my track, while I plotted several future targets to register with artillery and mortar fire. After all the Claymores and trip flares were in place, I would alert the platoon that I was going to call in "Def-Cons," or Defensive Concentrations which were actually target reference points for the artillery battery to shoot. If we were to get attacked at night, I would use those reference points to further direct the artillery fires into.

While all this combat-preparedness work was being accomplished in a very professional manner, Novell nonchalantly set up his Samsonite suitcase record player on the rear ramp of my track which was braced in a level position by a 5-gallon metal water can. From their place of special safekeeping, Novello retrieved his LP's, and loaded five of them on the spindle. Soon, the most melodic sound I had heard in months was softly emanating from the speakers, with a gorgeous voice asking, *"Do You Know the Way to San Jose?"* and sending a *"Message to Michael."* I had just been introduced to Dionne Warwick, right there in the middle of a very rough clearing in the jungle, smack dab in the middle of Vietnam, just before sunset. The ironic juxtaposition of the mud, the stench of the jungle, and the sounds of distant artillery explosions with the soft, lilting voice of Dionne Warwick made a lasting impression. To this day, each and every time I hear Dionne Warwick, I think back to the time when I first heard her, in a land so far away, but ever-present at least in my subconscience mind. And to Bruce Novello, my crazy medic and friend, I send a long overdue Thank You for this introduction to some beauty in the midst of our little war. Sadly, my note of Thanks to Bruce is too late for him to receive personally, as I learned recently that he died of cancer, related to exposure to Agent Orange. Once again, I'm reminded that sometimes our government is not our friend! Part of my personal credo has become: "I love my country, but I don't trust this government." With more and more of my Brothers in Arms being adversely impacted by Agent Orange, I'm distrusting my government even more. Rest in Peace, Bruce!

Anticipating Smoked Venison Sausage

DESPITE THE FACT that we were a mechanized infantry out-fit, the 2nd Battalion, (Mechanized) 47th Infantry, to be exact, the only mail that was normally delivered 'out in the field,' as it was called, was letter mail. Whoever made that decision must have failed to realize that an armored personnel carrier (APC) is in many ways, a rolling foot locker, so that there was no wont for plenty of space to hold all those packages that were now awaiting our return to Camp Bearcat and our battalion mail room. A week prior, I had received a very welcome letter from my Dad, informing me that a package of smoked-dry venison sausage would be there when we got back from our latest operation. Or so I hoped. My Dad had perfected a recipe for making sausage, and then had found a great smoke-house in Llano, Texas, to cure it and smoke it to preserve without refrigeration.

We had been operating in a jungle area southeast of Camp Bearcat, providing local security to a US Army Engineer unit, one equipped with Rome plows, - giant D-8 Caterpillars with a sharpened snag point on one end of their huge bull blade. The engineers' mission was to cut 100 meter-wide lanes through the triple-canopy jungle, lanes that began to be used as cart paths by the local folks on wood gathering missions, and lanes that might eventually become means for greater commerce in a developed South Vietnam. At least, that was the game plan and some of the long-term goals of a free and independent country. As we would learn later, keeping it free and independent became problematic because of a re-invasion by an aggressive northern neighbor.

So after completing the cut from Highway 15, due east to an intersection with another cut that headed due south towards *Ham Tan* on the coast, the Engineers started their long, slow withdrawal back to what passed for civilization – a warm shower instead of using an Australian shower bucket, a good hot meal instead of a B-3 unit out of the C-Ration case, and sleeping on a mosquito-net covered cot, with clean sheets, instead of a mosquito and leech-infested spot in the middle of the jungle. And our job was just about complete, as we guarded the Engineers and the loading of their huge jungle-eating machines on low-boys, for the slow drive back to their base camp in the *Long Binh* military complex.

At last, I could almost see the little hamlet through which we would pass before turning right onto Highway 15 and then on to Camp Bearcat. This little nondescript hamlet, like so many others in Vietnam, had not been overly friendly towards us on our trips through their narrow lanes. As a matter of fact, I distinctly remember hearing several shots coming from the hamlet, but never could identify a distinct target upon which to deliver a lethal response. Our company had been assigned to be the trail unit in the long convoy of APC's, self-propelled artillery pieces, engineer flatbeds, and assorted other vehicles in this vast accumulation of machinery. And my platoon was the trail unit of the entire batch, meaning that we were the last of the last.

Just as my last APC was entering the hamlet, I got a frantic call on my platoon radio net, informing me that one of the tracks had just 'broken a leg,' G.I. jargon that a major mechanical problem had occurred. Immediately, I radioed the company commander that we had a downed track, and that I would catch up with the convoy later. Returning to the disabled track, I noticed a complete absence of people in the hamlet, usually a very ominous sign that something bad was about to happen. After deploying my platoon into positions so that would allow us some local security, I examined the downed track, and saw that the rear idler wheel had been completely torqued off - a classic case of metal fatigue. The driver of this track already had his mechanic's tool kit out and was starting to remove some track pins and several blocks of track, thus shortening the track enough to loop it around the road wheels in a field-expedient way to regain a modicum of mobility. This "short-track" method would allow us to get back on the road, and to limp our way back to Camp Bearcat, but at a much slower pace than I wanted. A slow track is a much better target for Charlie. But my immediate concern was the seemingly deserted hamlet. Had I driven into an ambush site? Were my men in the middle of the kill zone or were they deployed strategically? Were the other platoons so far ahead that they wouldn't be able to come to my assistance if we got into a major fire fight? Were my men ready for any contingency that might arise?

Being assured by the track driver and an able-bodied mechanic that the track would be repaired as soon as humanly possible, I walked back to my track while checking on the security measures I had taken earlier. Everyone was in their proper position, ready for any attack that might come our way, with the possible exception of incoming mortars. All we had encountered in this area before were just some local VC, and I couldn't imagine them mortaring their own homes just to get to us. Inside my track, I rummaged around until found the remains of a box of hard candy that had been included in the weekly SP box we just received. This SP box contained cigarettes, bars of soap, toothpaste, stationery and a bag of individually wrapped hard candy, "Jolly Rogers," as I recall. I loaded my jungle fatigue shirt pockets with all the "Jolly Rogers" I could find, determined to give it away to any of the children in the hamlet, and provided of course they would show themselves. I ordered my Radio-Telephone Operator (RTO) to 'saddle up' and walk with me, in case I needed back-up.

Slowly strolling up the dirt path between my track and the 'downed pony,' I noticed some movement to my right front, a small little boy peeking furtively around the corner of his house. When we made eye contact, he ducked back behind the wall, and I quickly tossed a couple of Jolly Rogers in his general direction. He must have retrieved them, as soon another pair of eyes met mine, and another pair of Jolly Rogers was sent out in another peace gesture. Within five minutes, I was surrounded by all the children of the hamlet, each clamoring for a piece of candy. Slowly I maneuvered the crowd of children closer to where the mechanical repairs were happening, bribing them with my rapidly depleting source of candy. Having this happy crowd of children close to the mechanic would only increase the overall safety of my men, as no VC would dare shoot in our direction for fear of possibly hitting his own child. The youngest member of the hamlet – a diaper-less little boy – was being carried by his older sister, and I gestured that I wanted to hold the little boy. Already being a proud father of a little boy back home in the States, this seemed perfectly normal to me! I hasten to add that at this point in my life, I was the proud owner of a full, bulldog moustache, a rarity amongst the local villagers who were not so hirsute! The little boy was fascinated by my moustache, and finally worked up enough courage to touch it. In his excitement of this newfound wonder, he 'peed' all over my shirt, which made the crowd of children laugh nervously. I laughed along with them, as a little baby pee couldn't have made me smell any worse, having gone days without a shower! And besides, I didn't want to 'lose face' by acting embarrassed by this little accident of nature.

Seeing that the driver and mechanic had just about completed the 'short-track' procedure that would get us back on the road, I handed the little boy back to his older sister, and motioned my men to 'saddle up,' the signal to mount the tracks and get ready to move out. Back on the road again, my next stop, hopefully, was a small shop in *Long Thanh*, a village next to the entrance road to Camp Bearcat. I wanted to buy some baguettes, or what might reasonably pass for same, to accompany the long-awaited dried venison sausage. Next stop: the battalion mail room, after I got all my men squared away and had all the post-operation maintenance and security checks completed. Walking into the mail room, I was greeted by the unmistakable aroma of a German smokehouse, along with my friend the battalion supply officer, Leroy Brown. "Hey Barnes, is that your package that smells so good?" I couldn't deny the obvious, so I asked him if he could go mooch some cheese from the mess hall. "Roger that," was his excited reply, to which I responded, "Meet me in my hootch in 10 minutes!"

Soon we were enjoying the finest meal we had had in weeks – cheese, some freshly baked bread - *sans* the ever-present weevils - cold beer, and the best smoked venison sausage man could ever have wished for! Thanks, Pop, for your hunting skills, and your sausage-making expertise. Rest in Peace.

POST SCRIPT: During Operation *Just Cause* in Panama during the term of President George H.W. Bush, my son Greg was a member of the 75th Ranger Regiment, one of the US Army units dispatched to Panama to get rid of Manuel Noriega, the local dictator and chief drug exporter. Remembering how good that venison sausage tasted some 30+ years earlier, I asked my father if he had any dried sausage from the current harvest of deer. Fortunately for Greg, the Rangers were not in Panama long enough for an APO (Army Post Office) to be established, so the package was waiting for him when he returned from this mission. Soon SGT Greg was the most popular Ranger in his Ranger Company, as the aroma and flavors of venison sausage I had experienced in Vietnam were being replicated in Georgia. Three links of that Texas gourmet food were quickly devoured by some of the Army's finest – the Rangers! Thanks again, Pop, for that great sausage recipe, and for caring about your son and your grandson! And Thanks to the US Army Rangers for making the man my son is today.

Giving Away My War Trophies

"BRAVO 3-6, THIS is Tamale 1-5, over!" The radio call from our Forward Air Controller (FAC) broke the silence of that afternoon. 'Bravo 3-6' meant that I was the platoon leader of the 3rd Platoon, Company B, of our battalion, the 2nd Battalion (Mechanized) 47th Infantry. What made the call all the more startling was that Tamale 1-5 was actually a pilot in the Australian Air Force assigned to fly one of our 'Birddogs,' a small militarized Cessna that was loaded with radios and other avionics. As you can imagine, the FAC's main function was to guide the fast movers – F-4's, F-100's, and other jets – into those areas where we needed additional firepower and heavy ordnance. "Tamale 1-5, this is Panther Bravo 3-6!" I replied in my finest fake Australian accent I could muster. I was immediately greeted by "Alright mate, cut out the shit, I've got some Cong spotted for you! Willie Pete on the way!" "Willie Pete" was the GI acronym for 'white phosphorous,' which makes a very dense and concentrated area of white smoke when it hits the ground. With that advance warning, Tamale 1-5 nosed his Birddog over into a steep dive position, and fired a Willie Pete rocket into an area approximately 800 meters northwest of my position. We had been conducting a routine security patrol in this area without any contact with

GIVING AWAY MY WAR TROPHIES ❧

the VC, so the prospect of a firefight was not as remote as it first seemed. Quickly, I reconfigured my platoon into a more battle-ready formation and the heightened sense of danger became palpable. We set off on what was to become a history-making event.

Moving quietly through the jungle, we approached the spot where the Willie Pet rocket had hit earlier. Suddenly, M-16 and M-60 machinegun fire broke the silence. The men of Bravo 3-6 had made contact! Moving as quickly as possible to the point man, I asked him what was happening. "Two *Dinks* just broke and ran off! I didn't want to just run after them, as it might have been an ambush nearby!" Silently, I congratulated my point man for his good sense, and realized why I put him in that position in the first place. '*Dinks*' was a shortened version of '*dinky-dau*,' Vietnamese slang for 'crazy.' I immediately deployed my platoon in an inverted "V" formation, and started moving slowing in the direction that the point man said the VC had gone. We had only traveled about 50 feet when the left flank of the formation almost fell into the entrance hole of a tunnel. Nearby, we saw other signs that some VC had been there for quite a while, with a well-defined kitchen area, a small chicken pen with three chickens inside, racks for drying clothes, and other niceties of home. For the next three days, their home was going to be our home. And their chickens were going to be our next meal!

I ordered my tracks to start moving to my new location to provide more firepower; after a quick reconnaissance of the area, I was convinced that more than just two VC were guarding this area. I also called Bravo 6, my company commander CPT Tomlinson, and gave him a preliminary tally of what we had found. And after SGT Lawson, one of my squad leaders told me of what he had just found, I knew that I knew that I would be telling Bravo 6 much, much more, but would

prefer to do it in person. SGT Lawson, his fatigues now covered in the red mud of the wet laterite material of the area,
had just returned from exploring the first of many tunnels that
we would eventually discover, exploit and ultimately destroy.
His wide-eyed expression would only partially convey the
enormity of our discovery. "Sir, there are boxes and boxes of
ammo down there, and stuff I can't even identify! And I think
there are some land mines too. I only went into one room,
but the tunnel kept on going, and I could see that there were
many other rooms off the tunnel on either side of the main
tunnel!" With the prospects of us finding some legitimate war
trophies, it was becoming increasingly difficult keeping my
men out of the tunnels, and performing the security mission I
had assigned them to. "Everyone will get a damn war trophy,"
I assured them, "Now get back out there and stay alert! I expect Charlie just went to get some reinforcements, and he'll
be back soon!"

By now, I had two teams of two men each, back in the
tunnel complex, and their mission was to provide me with
a sketch of this subterranean treasure trove. One of my best
tunnel rats was Paul Ianni, whose small physical stature made
me wonder how he ever got drafted into the Army! But he
was indefatigable and always brought back the most accurate
information about the rooms in the total complex, and what
those rooms contained. What was beginning to emerge from
their drawings, descriptions and my own personal reconnaissance, was one long tunnel, extending approximately 100
meters, with huge rooms, measuring about 10' x 20', branch-
ing out from either side of the main tunnel, all filled with
weapons and ammunition of practically every conceivable
caliber and amount. The pucker factor was increasing by the
minute. This amount of war materiel was there for something
much bigger than the occasional VC squad we would only

occasionally encounter; this was at least sufficient to arm a regiment. Maybe more. Bravo 6, my company commander, and the other platoons of Company B couldn't get here soon enough for me.

A partial list of weapons found in this cache site included RPD light machineguns, PPSh-41's, sub-machineguns, SKS semi-automatic assault rifles, Mosin-Nagant 7.62mm sniper rifles, complete with 6-power telescopes, 12.7 mm heavy machineguns on tripods, 9mm Makarov pistols, 82 mm mortars, and 57 mm recoilless anti-tank guns. Not all of the weapons could qualify as a legitimate war trophy that we could bring back to the States, so the qualifying ones became closely guarded and coveted. I did manage to find a Browning 9mm pistol that I tagged for myself, and for some reason, I also tagged a Mosin-Nagant 7.62 mm sniper rifle for safe keeping, although I already had a good deer rifle at home. There seemed to be enough ammunition for every weapon to last for the world's longest firefight. We also discovered some medicines of French origin, with a manufacturing date of 1967. Our good ol' French allies! And documents that would only later reveal the true intent of the enemy and this cache site that we now possessed. The amount of ammunition was estimated to be between 600,000 and 800,000 rounds, with another 200+ anti-tank mines. The total weapons count was in the thousands. As it turned out, our discovery was the largest weapons and ammunition cache of the entire war. The documents that we discovered were translated and indicated that these weapons and ammunition were to be used in the attacks on Saigon. At the time, September-October 1967, Saigon was a relatively safe place, so the documents seemed very far-fetched to us. Only later were we to learn the true significance of this find, after experiencing the Tet Offensive and participating in the Tet Counter-Offensive.

Bravo 6 showed up, and after his preliminary inspection of the site, sent a report back to Battalion headquarters, requesting that the engineers and their Rome plows be diverted from their current mission, and to proceed to our little home to construct a landing zone. CPT Tomlinson knew that we were going to be here for quite a while, and that our resupply could only be accomplished by CH-47 helicopters which needed a large landing area. He underestimated the size of the LZ, as it eventually was large enough to land two CH-47's simultaneously, one being our resupply bird, the other one filled with reporters, photographers and assorted straphangers who came to see our find. One of the photographers snapped a picture of me near a large pile of rifles and sub-machineguns, just as I was adding another weapon to the pile. He was working for *Time* magazine, and I still have a copy of that photo, cut out of a magazine that my folks sent me! While this publicity couldn't hurt, my men, unbeknownst to me had nailed a cardboard sign, made out of a C-ration case to a nearby tree that read, "You have just been f**ked over by Bravo 3-6 and his merry men!" Thanks a lot, guys, for making me an even more conspicuous target! Months later, we found a sign in the general area, indicating that there was a $50,000 Vietnamese *dong* or piaster reward for me, Bravo 3-6, probably in response to our capturing and exploiting their weapons and ammunition cache. As I recall, $50,000 *dong* amounted to about $35 US! So much for my inflated view of myself! But that sign would have made a terrific war trophy today!

After all the weapons were removed from the subterranean rooms and properly inventoried, the next order of business was to get a fairly accurate count of the various types of ammunition which eventually would all be destroyed. Case after case of C-4 explosive was carried down into the tunnel complex by US Army Engineers, who had been flown in expressly for the purpose of providing explosive expertise. It was shaping up to be one hell of a bang! Each room in this complex was wired with block after block of C-4 placed on top of the crates of ammunition, with the C-4 daisy-chained together with detonation cord. The 'det' cord from each room was extended to the main tunnel and then connected to a line that went back to the tunnel entrance and eventually to the control panel where the Engineer captain would trigger the blast.

"Fire in the hole! Fire in the hole!" The standard pre-blast warning of all demolitions was sounded and broadcast over the radio, alerting everyone who needed to know what was about to happen. Although the noise wasn't as loud as I expected, the heaving and buckling and settling of the earth over the tunnel complex was much greater than anticipated. Once the dust, dirt and debris settled, we could see a large bowl-shaped indentation where the tunnel complex used to be, a depression in the earth that might have been replicated in the minds of the diggers of the complex itself, if only they could see our handiwork!

Several months later, our Battalion Maintenance Technician CW4 Bill Cunningham and I were sitting in my hootch, enjoying one of several rounds of adult beverages. Bill was scheduled to catch the "Freedom Bird" back to the 'world' the next morning. Chief Cunningham had been an absolute miracle worker, somehow keeping our ancient armored personnel carriers repaired and running, often working as hard and getting as dirty as his well-trained mechanics. His ability to diagnose and repair our equipment was legendary. "You know, I've been out there with you guys in the field, but never got a chance to get a war trophy." Although his speech was somewhat slurred by one too many Scotches, I understood him perfectly well. Reaching behind me and opening my wall locker, I pulled out my own war trophy, a carefully wrapped Mosin-Nagant sniper rifle, complete with 6-power telescope, handed to Bill, and said, "Now you've got a war trophy! Get home and kill that deer you've been hunting for so long!" However, the next day, before leaving for the 90th Replacement Detachment, where we were all processed through on our way in and out of Vietnam, Bill stopped by my hootch, and handed the rifle back to me. "I think that was Scotch talking last night, so I won't hold you to it, and here's your rifle back." Refusing the rifle, I told Bill that I knew perfectly well what I was doing the night before and insisted that he use it as we discussed.

Returning to Camp Bearcat after exploiting that weapons and ammunition cache, I had complied with the 9th Infantry Division Directive that all qualifying war trophies by registering and keeping these weapons at the 9th Military Police Company's office until DEROS time. So being a good, obedient officer, I tagged my beautiful Browning 9mm pistol and surrendered it to some MP clerk who began lusting after my prize. In retrospect, it's a good thing I didn't register the sniper rifle too! On the day before I was to report to the 90th Replacement Detachment or 90th Repl Depl as we called it, for my flight back home, I went to the office of the 9th Military Police and showing my receipt, requested my pistol. "What pistol?" was the response, and then I knew that some MP just found himself in possession of my war trophy, and I had my second good reason for not liking military police. Making the flight back home was more important than my Browning 9mm pistol, so I accepted this reality and headed to *Long Binh*. Through a strange and wonderful set of circumstances, in 1987, I was given a brand new 9mm pistol by my NCO's of a battalion I once had the honor of commanding, and this pistol means so much more to me than that other 9mm ever could! But I still don't like MP's!

Some 19 months later, at the beginning of my second tour in Vietnam, I was enjoying my last night of peace and quiet before assuming command of my rifle company, and decided that one more greasy hamburger and cold beer was in order at the nearby Officers' Club. As I walked in the front door, there stood good ol' Bill Cunningham, regaling some earlier arrivals of his hunting prowess! After the hugs and back-slapping had subsided, I asked Bill about the rifle and that pesky buck back home. "Nailed his ass at 400 yards! Got his head mounted above my fireplace, just where he belongs, thanks to that rifle you gave me," Bill related.

So Thank You again, Bill Cunningham for all you did in keeping our old war wagons running. You gave me a perfect example of what a maintenance technician really looks like. You made better use of that rifle than I could have! And Thanks to the various mechanics who labored tirelessly to keep us as mobile as possible! Finally, Thank You, Paul Ianni, for being the best tunnel rat I could ever have prayed for!

Gifts in Small Bottles

ONE OF THE good things about being in a mechanized infantry battalion is that we could carry extra goodies in them instead of having to carry them on our backs, like the straight-leg grunts had to do. We could stow extra uniforms, more ammunition, more water, occasionally cases of beer, letters from home, and other necessities or niceties. When we were out on operations, the resupply bird, a Chinook C-47 helicopter, would bring in two blivets of fuel, one MOGAS, the other diesel, slung underneath the copter, and internally, letter mail, ammo, water, sometimes a hot meal, but no packages of goodies from "home," our term for the United States of America. If we were working with a combat engineer unit, they would use their bulldozers to create a large pile of dirt inside our temporary compound, and the blivets of fuel would be positioned there first, in order to refuel the various vehicles using gravity instead of using a hand-pump.

One of the bad things about being in a mechanized infantry battalion is that the official Army Postal Office policy was that no packages from home would be delivered to troops in the field. As with many "official declarations," this one also failed the Common Sense and Logic test. Sometimes we would have to wait for weeks before we could get the "goodies" that our loved ones had sent us, little things gastronomic treats that would help us eat the C-rats, little things that helped us stay clean, or little treats that could help us remember the finer things in life, like a stiff drink!

We had been involved in Operation Santa Fe, a joint operation with the 169th Combat Engineer Battalion, providing security as the engineers but wide swaths through the jungle, or "rain forest" as the tree-huggers are fond of calling it. These 100-meter wide cuts were designed to facilitate mechanized or armored forces' movement between national highways or strategic points of interests, thereby helping to pacify the countryside. As a negative, these land cuts also allowed Charlie to move more easily, at least at night if he dared, and that caused us to position night ambush sites in certain locations. Clearing all of the vegetation, all the way down to the bare earth, created two curses for us Grunts: extremely sticky mud in the rainy season, and chocking clouds of dust in the dry season. Little by little, I was beginning to more fully understand the meaning of the phrase, "War is Hell!" What we didn't know then, but are realizing now with growing degrees of mortality, it that those same areas of the jungle were later sprayed with Agent Orange. They would become an area visited many times by men of the 2nd Battalion. With the ever-growing number of diseases and conditions ascribed to Agent Orange, and with the increasing numbers of early deaths of Vietnam Veterans, in many respects, our government became our enemy. Maybe this would be an appropriate epitaph for Lyndon Baines Johnson and all the other morons that were involved in the decision-making process to employ Agent Orange.

Sometimes the security mission for the bulldozers and the Rome plows required us to dismount our tracks and patrol in the jungle, providing flank security for the Engineers. For the uninitiated, a Rome plow was basically a D-8 Caterpillar with a modified push-blade in front called a 'stinger' blade. These heavily-armored bulldozers took their name from the town of Rome, Georgia, where they were made. Using the 'stinger' blade, the operators would tear away large chunks of the tree trunk until it was weak enough to be pushed over, when another bulldozer would shove it over to the edge of the clearing, and the process was repeated over and over again until a long rough trail was cut through primordial jungle.

Even though I had only been in country less than two months, I already had two different company commanders. The first one, whose name shall go unmentioned, had been relieved for incompetence by the battalion commander, and now, a very senior first lieutenant had been named as the interim commander. 1LT Alex L. Posluszny had arrived in Vietnam with the other original warriors who had formed up the Battalion back at Ft. Riley, Kansas, and had already served as the Scout Platoon Leader. He was a battle-tested soldier, a product of Alfred University, which he attended on a basketball scholarship, and judging by his lanky frame, I suspect he was a good basketball player. In one instance of self-deprecation, Alex told us about his basketball coach, a man given to sarcasm as a motivational tool. During one particular practice, the ball was passed to Alex, who was supposed to feed it to the man charging in for a lay-up, but the ball carelessly slipped through his hands, hence no lay-up shot. When the coach's shrill whistle quit ringing is his ears, Alex heard the coach say, "Hey, Pos, have you heard from your hands lately?" But none of Alex's faculties or extremities was questioned, as he successfully led us through several months of operations, all missions accomplished. On one particular mission, the company command post had received a cryptic message from our S-2, or Intelligence Officer: "We have received a report that there is a VC company in your area; this message is rated as 'B-2'!" The alpha-numeric coding system for intelligence reports was based on a matrix of Reliability and Probability. The 'Reliability' of the message was the alpha part, and related to the reliability of the source of the information. The numeric part or the 'Probability' part pertained to the likelihood of the message. Although I never saw or heard about an "A-1" message during either of my tours in Vietnam, I would assume that you just had to start shooting, as Charlie was that close! But a B-2 definitely increased the pucker factor. It was the highest I had ever heard about.

We were in an area of very dense jungle, with the tracks within 50 meters of the tree line. A small area had been cleared and all of the tracks of Company B occupied this patch of ground. No other line companies or any supporting troops were within 2 kilometers or clicks, as we called them. Alex had assembled us platoon leaders in his track, and gave us the following instructions. "Put out triple the normal number of Claymores and trip flares tonight, with at least six wires for every track. Do the same thing with the supplemental positions between the tracks. Brief your platoons – all of your men – we're going to be blowing Claymores all night long. Charlie knows we're here, as you can't camouflage a company of tracks very well so we can't fool him. But we can throw him off-balance about where to try to attack us if we keep an irregular pattern of explosions going off. When you hear a Claymore going off on the opposite side of the perimeter where you are, wait 10 minutes and blow one on your side. Of course, if you detect movement in your sector, hit the Claymores and don't wait for the 10 minute interval. If that Claymore doesn't do the trick, open up with the .50's! You know the drill - just execute what you've learned. Any questions?"

Few people in Bravo Company got any sleep that night,

but all of us made it through to fight yet another day. The next morning, we could see the damage that the 50 or so Claymores had done to the vegetation from ground level to about four feet off the ground. If Charlie had been in the area, at least he had to good sense to avoid the exploding ring of fire that we presented that night, and he would live to fight another day. Or night. The fighters of the elusive 273rd VC Battalion and Company B would meet again on the battlefield sometime in the future, this time with fatal results for both parties. But for the warriors of Company B, good news came in the form of a message from Panther 33, the Net Control Station for the Battalion, relaying an order from Panther 6, to return to Bearcat.

As with every return to the basecamp at Bearcat, one of the most important chores was to visit the Battalion Mail Room and see if any packages from home had arrived. The sounds of joy were directly proportional to the quantity of the goodies with any given package. I was sharing my package of home-made oatmeal cookies with my fellow platoon leaders when a message came to me by a runner: "Bravo 6 needs to see you at his hootch right away!" Crap! What did I do now, or what crummy mission had my platoon pulled now, or what was the problem, I thought to myself. Entering Bravo 6's hootch, I was greeted by a smiling Alex Posluszny, holding an open box of miniature liquor bottles of every imaginable flavor and origin! His father, it seemed, worked for one of the major airlines in the States as a maintenance supervisor. Part of his responsibilities included an inspection of the interior of the aircraft, and in the process, had accumulated a rather stellar collection of bottles, the contents of which we were about to enjoy. "Here's to more Claymores!" Alex offered an excellent toast to that little weapon that had contributed to our enjoyment and safety of that particular moment.

Thank you, 1LT Alex Posluszny, for sharing that little bit luxury in the midst of the paragon of uncivilization, also known as war. Later in life, Alex suffered through a series of heart-disease related incidents, and was not able to attend any of the Regimental Reunions. Like many of our fellow Brothers in Arms, he died too soon, probably another victim of Agent Orange. But at least I thank him posthumously for being a great leader at a very trying time in Vietnam. May your soul continue to rest peace, as you deserve your place in Paradise!

Nurses and Sleeping in a Jeep

ONE OF THE many benefits of being in the 9th Infantry Division, particularly the 2nd Battalion, 47th Infantry (Mechanized), was being relatively close to the *Long Binh* Logistics base and all its goodies, to *Bien Hoa* Air Base for those going on various R&R trips, and to the 24th Evacuation Hospital. Being a mechanized outfit, we would have to get major end-items replaced for our aging fleet of mechanized beasts, which were rapidly approaching the end-of-life as we know it, due to excessive use, various battle damages, and simple wear and tear. Since a Corps-level maintenance facility was there at *Long Binh*, we were able to acquire those necessary parts more readily, and thanks to the stupendous efforts of our battalion maintenance section, our armored beasts kept performing.

Long Binh also had a great PX – Post Exchange to you civilians – and often, they had items long before our little PX at Camp Bearcat could ever get them, if they ever got them at all. Back in those days, the "high-tech" audio stuff was reel-to-reel tape decks and I was determined to get the best system I could afford. If I could find a worthy tape per month, I'd buy it, since it was about all I could afford on my meager income, since I was sending 95% of it home for my wife and child. And this pay process was a nightmare for the first four months of my tour; my wife would have to go to our bank, and get a 30-day loan to cover the bills until the glorious US Army Finance team got around to sending her a check, at which time she would pay off the loan, and wait for the next month. Fortunately, we had a good relationship with Mr. Banker, and by the end of the third month, all my wife had to do was make a telephone call, and money would be placed into our account, as the banker knew that we would pay it off when Uncle Sam paid us! Today, things are automated, and our warriors today don't have the financial hassles that beset us in the 60's and 70's!

For the non-Hawai'i-bound soldiers going on R&R, *Bien Hoa* Air Base was the place to go for free flights to all the other R&R sites – Hong Kong, Sydney, Australia, Kuala Lumpur, Malaysia, and the Philippines. As I was to find out later on my second tour, getting a 'hop' on a MAC-charter flight was as easy as standing in line with a proper set of orders, even if those orders were hand-made! More on that felonious activity later!

One of my fellow platoon leaders in Bravo Company was 1LT Warren Clair, a tall, lanky, good-natured fellow from Ohio. Before he left the States, Clair had been dating a very attractive nurse, and apparently, the attraction was mutual, as she later voluntarily joined the Army, and was ultimately stationed at the 24th Evacuation Hospital in *Long Binh*. Or maybe she was just stalking him, I don't know! So it was only fitting that during a lull in combat operations, our Battalion was having some good down time at Camp Bearcat when Clair asked our Company Commander, 1LT Alex Posluszny if he could go to *Long Binh* to see his girlfriend. Since it was not prudent to travel alone anywhere in Vietnam, Clair asked me if I wanted to go with him. The prospects of seeing a 'round-eye' woman after several months in the jungle were alluring enough, just to sit and talk to one, much less any other action! So off to *Long Binh* we went, still fully armed, clothed and equipped for combat, but travelling in a jeep! I really felt quite naked, not having my armored personnel carrier underneath me!

When we arrived at the 24th Evac Hospital, the shift change as about to happen, so we waited in our jeep, anticipating being invited into their Officers' Club for some adult beverages and whatever else came our way. Clair introduced me to his girlfriend and a couple of other nurses, but after a round of drinks, he and his lady friend disappeared. Imagine that! Being a happily married man at the time, I remembered my wedding vows, even after being plied with really good Scotch whisky by some really good looking women!

About an hour later, Clair rejoined me at the Officers' Club, but by this time, it was way too late to attempt a drive back down Highway 15 to Camp Bearcat. My momma raised ugly children, not dummies! I made a radio call back to the Tactical Operations Center – the TOC – to inform them that we were going to RON – Remain Over Night – at the 24th Evac, and would be back in the morning. Naturally, there were no 'Visiting Officers' Quarters' at the 24th Evac, so we did the only thing available, sleep in the jeep! Unless you have ridden in a jeep for any length of time, you can't really appreciate the abject comfortless condition of this vehicle. Needless to say, it wasn't designed for sleeping. But we would take turns sleeping on the hood until it got too cold, then we would crank up the jeep for a few minutes and enjoy the heat from the engine, until the cold woke us up again, then we'd switch positions and repeat the process! By the time sunrise woke us up from our troubled sleep, we were more than ready to hit the road back to Camp Bearcat. Aching from having to curl up on the hood, or from trying to sleep sitting up, we finally made it back to Camp Bearcat in time for a good breakfast. I decided right then and there that if Clair ever asked me again to visit his girlfriend that I would develop a severe case of something and would beg off. Like the monkey said after making love to a skunk, "I don't want to appear ungrateful, but I know when I've had enough!" So Thank You, Warren Clair, for inviting me on that eventful trip to the 24th Evac, and for that brief respite from the rigors of war!

My Introduction to Victoria Bitter

IMMERSION FOOT WAS and still is the scourge of the storied grunt, a medical condition that could render an infantry unit combat ineffective without a shot being fired in their direction. This plague of the foot soldier was not discovered in Vietnam, as I'm sure our fathers enjoyed the same set of conditions of constantly wet feet, high heat in the jungles of the Pacific Theatre of Operations. In colder climes, this malady was called 'trench foot,' reflecting one of the more immemorial aspects of World War I, trench warfare and its attendant misery. But the outcome was the same – large blisters, rotting flesh, and in the worst of cases, loss of toes.

So it became imperative for commanders to constantly assess the conditions of their men's feet, and to have the courage to tell the next higher-ups that their unit was not fit for combat, when that threshold was crossed. Sometimes, junior officers, too much driven by visions of higher rank, eschewed the condition of their command, and declared the men ready to fight, when in fact, the platoon or company was sorely in need of a few more days of drying out. Somehow, God gave me enough wisdom, at least on a temporary basis, to keep my mouth shut as an FNG and to learn from the men I now had to honor of leading. Most of the men of the 3rd Platoon,

Company B, had been in country for six months before I took over. They had been through some intense fighting up in the Iron Triangle, had acquitted themselves admirably, and had helped the 2ⁿᵈ Battalion earn high marks from the Brigade and Division commanders. What I learned from some of the "old-timers" is that the feet had to be kept dry, as conditions allowed, and one of the best ways to do this was by not wearing the heavy woolen socks Uncle Sam issued to us. While it took some getting used to, soon I was able to develop the necessary callouses to guard my bare feet against blisters while going sockless. Thankfully, I never developed any symptoms of the dreaded immersion foot.

For an all too brief period of time in the summer of 1967, the 2ⁿᵈ Battalion, 47ᵗʰ Infantry (Mechanized) had the distinct pleasure of conducting joint operations with an Australian cavalry squadron in *Phuoc Tuy* Province. Since this operation was in the middle of the rainy season, keeping one's feet dry all the time was not just problematic but downright impossible. I had learned that my feet would dry out much quicker if I didn't wear socks, since the thick cotton/wool socks issued by Uncle Sam were notorious for sucking up water and keeping it, being a major contributor to the conditions of immersion foot. As long as I kept the majority of the mud out of the drainage holes on the boots, my feet would usually dry out overnight when I could take my boots off. With much of the upper part of the boot being constructed of ballistic nylon, the drying process was accelerated over the older all-leather boots. These innovations were not available in the combat boots worn by our Australian brethren, and the negative results were apparent.

The Australian Cavalry Squadron was probably the best performing member of the allied coalition that fought in Vietnam. Other coalition members, which included a medical team from the Philippines, a mechanized unit from Thailand, and a Republic of Korea infantry division rounded out the allied forces in Vietnam, helping the ARVN in their fight against communist aggression, terrorism and insurgency. Like many civil service workers, the Filipinos just seemed to work enough to get by without over-exerting themselves, irrespective of the great need in the local population for better medical care. The Thais were all about appearances, with their perfectly tailored uniforms, the perfectly washed APC's, and their perfectly inept approach to conducting an effective counter-insurgency. Because of their failure to adopt the latest techniques and tactics of defeating the enemy, the Thais suffered too many battle casualties, far in excess of the number of corresponding VC losses. But they looked good dying. The ROK's brought their form of personal discipline, bordering on brutality, with them from Korea. Apparently their mindset was by applying the same form of discipline that was frequently meted out to members of their ranks, they could 'win the battle of the hearts and minds' of the local folks and hence the VC. They seemed to personify that adage about "using a sledge hammer to kill flies," a system that hasn't work yet. One has to think if this was some of the tactic used more recently in Iraq and Afghanistan, which really was the same game of hearts and minds, but a different geographical location. And in keeping with creating an entirely new dictionary for military jargon, the 21st century term for what we did in the 60's and 70's is now called "asymmetrical warfare." Um hmm. More words games.

But the Australian fighting men were different and better. It really wasn't a matter of racial preferences, but the fact that they were better soldiers, from tactics to maintenance procedures, to being able to adopt new techniques in how to fight our very elusive enemy. Visiting a platoon of the Aussie's in anticipation of another phase of our operations, I soon discovered that immersion foot was an international malady, afflicting the Diggers as much as the Americans. My counter-part was a lieutenant of Scottish descent, and adding that Scottish brogue to the Australian accent almost made meaningful communications impossible! Guarding against any possible misunderstanding or miscommunication, I asked his platoon sergeant to be an interpreter just in case! Naturally the weather became a matter of conversation, and it was then I learned that his platoon had been hit hard by immersion foot and would only have about half his men ready to go. I asked him if he would like some jungle boots to replace the all-leather boots issued to the Aussie Army. Answering in the definite affirmative, I dispatched my platoon sergeant to go to Camp Bearcat and return with as many serviceable pairs of jungle boots that he could find. Early in my military career, I learned not to ask sergeants where they acquire things, but rarely was I disappointed with the results after sending an NCO on a scrounging mission. I figured it was none of my business where they wondrously and miraculously acquire the necessary items; besides which, I later learned that by not knowing, I couldn't be charged with being an 'accessory after the fact.' My own personal felonious acts would emerge later!

Sure enough, SSG Amaral returned on the next resupply Chinook with sacks of letter mail, three FNG's, and two duffel bags of jungle boots. These boots were in various stages of serviceability, ranging from brand new to well-worn but still useable. After loading the two duffle bags into my APC, we made a quick drive over to the Aussie compound to make our contribution to the improved health condition of our Digger brothers. Their gratitude was palpable, and took the form of barbecue and exceptionally cold beer, in a way that Aussie warriors did best. One sip of that marvelous Aussie brew, and I was immediately jealous of their ability to import and enjoy a truly good-tasting beer, instead of the leftovers from the marketing wars back in the US that we were forced to consume. Such was my enjoyment of Victoria Bitter that I had to prove it myself with three more cans of that lovely quaff! Thank You, our Australian allies, for your spectacular successes in Vietnam, your gracious if not downright rowdy hospitality, and your sense to bring some really great beer with you to Vietnam!

In 2009, I finally got to fulfill one of my "bucket list" items by going to Australia to see my brother. Bill, the middle of us three Barnes brothers, had moved there in 1973 after believing that the USA was doomed to destruction with the election of Richard Nixon, such is the warped thinking of the liberal mind. Bill had served in the Peace Corps in the early 60's, and on returning to the States from a 3-year stint in Turkey, and was quite eligible for the draft, irrespective of the fact that he had served his country well there. I was already commissioned by that time, and realizing what the war in Vietnam was all about, at least from a tactical perspective, decided to volunteer for Active Duty from my safe Army National Guard position, for a variety of reasons, one being the distinct purpose of keeping my brother out of Vietnam. If he had been drafted, the worse that would have happened to him would have been a tour in Korea, since the Army wouldn't send two brothers to a combat zone at the same time unless they volunteered for it. At one point in time, I had a pair of brothers assigned to the Scouts, but they were both volunteers. Don't get me wrong, I love my brother, but he's a real klutz and too hard-headed to mold into a person who could have put up with the rigors of fighting in the jungle, and I didn't want him coming home in a rubber bag.

Not only did I get to spend some quality time with my

klutzy brother and his rather dysfunctional family, but I got to play a great round of golf at one of the many municipal golf courses in the Adelaide area. I was also given a personally guided tour of the South Australia Army Museum, where I learned of the very significant contributions they made to the Allied success in World War II. On the flight back to the States after my 3-week stay, the Qantas stewardess ask for my choice of a glass of wine, or a can of Victoria Bitter before dinner. So in the interests of maintaining proper contact with my past, I opted for the latter, and enjoyed it as much as the first one in Vietnam! So Thank You again, my Australian warrior brothers, for first introducing me to your wonderful beer! And Thank You, brother Bill, for your wonderful hospitality!

Convoy Permits? We Don't Need No Stinkin' Permits

COMPLYING WITH THE Battalion Standing Operating Procedures (SOP), every member of my platoon wore his steel pot – 'helmet' to the civilians – and flak jacket, every time we were riding on our armored personnel carriers (APC's or 'tracks' as we called them). Adding this weight and bulk only exacerbated the heat and humidity of the rainy season, but rules is rules, as they say, and if the flak jacket could help slow down or stop a bullet, it was worth the discomfort. The flak jacket also covered up my rank of lieutenant on my collar.

And so properly attired, we were heading back to Camp Bearcat, after finishing a spectacularly uneventful 30 days, chasing the elusive 273rd Viet Cong Battalion. It seems that ever since coming into country, all I ever heard about was how bad this VC unit was, how they had always eluded contact with a superior American unit. Frankly, I was beginning to doubt they ever existed. I was looking forward to a hot meal, a warm shower, and a cold beer, when my company commander called, informing us that another American unit, the 2nd Battalion, 39th Infantry, had made contact with the infamous 273rd VC Battalion, and was heavily engaged in a pitched battle. Our new mission was to provide whatever firepower and assistance we could, to hopefully render this enemy force combat ineffective. So much for the hot meal, the warm shower, and the cold beer, at least for now!

After receiving this distracting news, I relayed the same info to my other tracks, and the pace was immediately increased as my driver Vance pushed our old war wagon to its maximum speed. One of the things I later learned about my driver was that he had been a mechanic on a professional hot rod team in California, and knew the automotive workings of our APC's as well as our mechanics. I also learned that my APC was one of the fastest in the Battalion, thanks to Vance's prowess. Because our internal communications on the track didn't work, I had to sit on the driver's hatch cover, immediately behind my driver, and relay my driving instructions to him via succinct taps on his helmet. A tap on the right side indicated my intent for him to turn right, and a tap on the opposite side of his helmet meant go left. A tap on top meant go forward, with the speed being measured by the intensity of the tap.

By the time that my instructions had been relayed to my squad leaders commanding the tracks behind me, we were just entering the huge logistical and command and control base of *Long Binh*. This enormous complex of various military headquarters, including United States Army Vietnam, better known as USARV, the 1st Signal Brigade, II Field Forces, 1st Logistics Command, and many others, consisted of miles of paved or semi-paved roads, hundreds of buildings of innumerable shapes and sizes, and home of some of the most obnoxious Military Policemen this side of the Pecos river. Knowing the seriousness of the situation with our brother warriors in the 2-39th Infantry, we drove at the top speed that our ancient tracks would allow. Speeding through *Long Binh*, even at the breath-taking speed of 30 mph, I was surprised to see an MP jeep pull up beside me, with the occupant on the passenger side frantically waving me over and motioning me to stop. Pulling on the back of Vance's collar to indicate "Stop," we pulled over to the side of the road, with the MP jeep stopping right in front of my track, about 10' ahead of us.

After climbing down the front of my track, I was met by this pudgy little MP Sergeant, whose swagger and demeanor announced a person who was consumed with the "Little Man" syndrome. "Where's your Convoy Permit?" he insolently asked. Pulling my flak jacket open to expose my silver bar, I responded, "You mean, 'where's your Convoy Permit, SIR'?" He quickly delivered the sloppiest salute I've ever seen, and properly repeated his question. "Where's your Convoy Permit, SIR?" My immediate and heated response was, "I don't have a Convoy Permit, I don't need a convoy Permit, and in case you haven't figured it out, there's a war going on down the road, and I've been ordered to participate in it! Now when I climb back up on my track and tap my driver on his helmet, you'd better have your jeep out of my way, or we'll run over it!" There were several, very colorful expletives shouted in the foregoing lecture, but in the interest of common decency, have been omitted here.

Climbing back up the front slope of my track, I sat down behind Vance and noticed that the little fat sergeant was getting back into the passenger side of his jeep. True to my word, I tapped Vance on the top of his helmet, and my track started forward, just as the MP jeep was attempting to move further to the side of the road. The right front part of my track nudged the left rear bumper of the jeep, pushing it into the drainage ditch. Apparently, Vance had overheard the entire conversation between the MP and me, and took me at my word. Good ol' Vance! But by now, I knew that the little fat sergeant was screaming into his radio, filing his report with higher headquarters of how he had been assaulted by some nasty malcontented Grunts who ignored his demands for a Convoy Permit!

Five miles later down Highway 15, I received another radio message from Bravo 6, informing me that the 273rd VC Battalion had broken contact with the 2-39th Infantry. Maybe that hot meal, warm shower, and cold beer wasn't so distant after all! But then I remembered the run-in, no pun intended, with the little fat MP Sergeant, and how I would have to try to explain my way out of this predicament.

Arriving at the our Battalion area, and after insuring that all post-operation actions had been completed and my men were on the way to the Mess hall, I immediately sought out our Battalion Commander to give him my version of what happened before less reasonable men got to his ear. I was anticipating a serious ass-chewing at the very least, with possibly greater punishment, depending on the tainted testimony of the little fat sergeant. Locating LTC Moreland in his office, I reported to him, and told him my version of the incident, trying not to leave out anything except the colorful expletives. LTC Moreland listened attentively, not interrupting once. When I was finished, he picked up his telephone and called the commander of the 525th Military Police Battalion, parent headquarters of the offensive little fat sergeant. Once contact with the other commander was made, LTC Moreland commenced to render a stern lecture to the other commander, informing him that the 2-47th (Mechanized) didn't need any stinkin' Convoy Permits, and telling the MP command to quit harassing his warriors. The lecture was actually more colorful than this, but again in the interests of decent company, the colors are hereby omitted! LTC Moreland hung up the telephone, turned back to me and said with a huge smile, "I think that takes care of that, don't you?" Thanking him profusely for covering for my youthful indiscretion, I saluted him and promptly made a mental note of how commanders – good commanders – take care of their troops. I reminded myself that telling him the truth, the whole, plain, unvarnished truth was the best policy, and promising myself that if I ever had the good fortune of being a commander at his level, that I would take care of my subordinates with all the grace and common sense that I had just been party to. Thank you LTC Arthur Moreland, for that thoughtful mentoring lesson that later served me well! Now Rest in Peace, you have earned your reward. And thank you, Stanley Vance, for being the best driver in Company B!

The Pineapple Girl

AS MY FADING memory best recalls, *Vung Tau* was a tropical paradise on the coast of Vietnam, complete with tree-lined street with old French colonial houses, a clean sandy beach, and only a minimal military presence. Sadly, the houses looked like they had never seen any repairs since the French retreated back to the land of *brie, pate foie gras,* and their manufacturing of surrender flags, with their cowardly tails tucked between their spindly legs. If you've guessed that I don't care for the French or their conduct as a colonial power, just reach back and pat yourself on the back for the correct answer! Unlike the British, the French left a legacy prostitutes, taxi drivers, and thieves. Maybe because of the French history of duplicity, *Vung Tau* was also the in-country R&R site for the Viet Cong, at least that was the *rumeur du jour,* and that was one of the reasons why it was so safe there.

So why was I in *Vung Tau,* the In-Country R&R (Rest and Recreation) site? I had been "on the line" since late May 1967, and had just completed the exploitation of the largest arms and ammunition cache yet discovered in the entire war; as it later turned out, this claim was never bettered by any other unit or discovery. It just so happened that MAJ Ray Funderburk, the 9th Infantry Division Public Affairs Officer, was not only a good journalist, but knew how to write a story that would bring some long-overdue credit to the Division. Being one of the last of the major units to be deployed into Vietnam, the 9th had to play catch-up in the area of military success stories, noteworthy events, and awards and decorations for worthy warriors. In fact, one of the earlier Division Commanders didn't think awards were all that necessary, thinking instead that the soldiers were just doing their job, irrespective of the heroics involved. It was not until the tenure of Major General Julian J. Ewell that the Division started having an active "Awards and Decorations" program worthy of the multiple deeds of valor with the Division. Ray Funderburk played a hugely important role in that PR battle, and was destined to play a much more active and heroic role in a future battle. His contributions and successes that the Scouts experienced will be noted in a later vignette. So significant were Funderburk's actions on 31 January 1968 that he is one of the few people who has been made an "Honorary Scout."

And I had just been ordered to take a 3-day R&R trip to *Vung Tau*, partially in response and reward to my platoon's discovery and exploitation of this cache and partially because I was simply exhausted and emaciated after surviving a week-long stay at the 24th Evacuation Hospital with "fever of unknown origin," or FOUO for the official medical records. Apparently, the Army tried to treat every fever as a pathological manifestation of malaria, and when the usual treatment had no effect, the resultant diagnosis was FOUO. My later research into the symptoms revealed this FOUO to be more likely a case of dengue fever, a debilitating, mosquito-borne disease that has several malarial-like symptoms, but without the malarial smear in blood samples. Dengue fever causes one's intestines to reject any form of nutriment, sustenance, or liquid, and demonstrates this rejection in the vilest and frequent manner you can imagine. It was also referred to as 'having the 360's,' as both ends were in revolt. Emerging from the hospital, I strongly resembled a person who had just been freed from a Nazi starvation experiment.

Arriving in *Vung Tau* from a flight on an Air America C-46, I realized only later that the opportunity to ride this ol' bird was historic enough! There still may be airlines that fly this ancient aircraft, but I probably can't even pronounce the name of the country. But the short hop from *Bien Hoa* Air Base to *Vung Tau* avoided the long, dusty and sometimes dangerous ride down *Quoc Lo* or National Highway 15. The local taxi took me to the near-by Officers' Club, where I was assigned a nice, clean room, complete with air-conditioner, a real bed with clean sheets on it, and access to a warm-water shower. It was almost as if I had died and gone to Heaven! Standing next to the Registration Desk was a row of slot machines, so with my newly acquired roll of nickels, I proceeded to try my luck with the one-armed-bandits. My luck in the jungle, or as the politically correct call it, "the tropical rain forest," had been good up until now, so maybe Lady Luck was going to be with me tonight. Or at least this afternoon! Sure enough, I hit a jackpot, enough to pay for my room, a few meals, and a taxi ride to the beach.

Entering the Dining Room of the Officers' Club, I was immediately struck by the length and largess of the salad bar! Practically every sort and variety of edible vegetable was present, and I was quickly reminded of the fact that fresh salads had become a distant memory, as we were never treated to any of this gourmet food while we were in the field. But here in the Officers' Club, the normal process for visitors was to find a place at a table, wait for the Vietnamese waitress to take your order for your entrée of choice, and then proceed to the salad bar. Or in my case, multiple trips to the salad bar.

And for those Saigon Warriors sitting at another table in their sterilized and starched khakis, staring at me and my well-worn jungle fatigues with such disdain, they would get their comeuppance in a few months, as things turned out.

What I found to be truly amazing was how good sea water feels on leech bites, mosquito bites and other assorted scratches and cuts! Other GI's were just strolling on the beach, enjoying the gentle waves, or simply relaxing, something that none of us had probably done in the last 6-7 months or however long we had been in country. How could we completely relax and let our guard down, when one never really knew the loyalties of the local folks? For example, I learned later on that one of the barbers at the 9th Infantry Division Base at Bearcat, was caught trying to emplace a claymore mine on a road leading to the main entrance. Even here, in the alleged dual R&R site of Allied forces and Viet Cong forces, I never could really completely let go and relax, but the really cold beer in my hand was helping as much as it could.

Walking down the beach was a young Vietnamese girl, about 10 years old I'm guessing, with a basket of pineapples on either end of the pole resting on her shoulder. These were not the same sized pineapple of Hawaiian or Costa Rican origin, but smaller, and as I was soon to learn, much sweeter. So she and I bargained for the purchase price, and once agreed upon, her magic fingers began manipulating the odd-shaped knife as the peeling fell away in one long piece. Holding the pineapple top as a handle, she gave it to me with a shy smile. One bite later, I was convinced that I would buy another delicious morsel from this little beachside merchant, but first, a quick dip in the bay to wash off the pineapple juice! The second pineapple was just as good as the first, but the price was a little higher, as I realized that the bounty from the slot machines was more than I needed, and the pineapple girl of

Vung Tau needed the money more than I did. I kept remembering that I was a guest in her country, and would probably leave the following May, hopefully intact, while she would have to stay here to whatever fate would have in store for her.

Looking back some 40+ years later, I wonder whatever happened to her, while still being eternally grateful for that brief and delicious encounter on the beaches of *Vung Tau*. One of the items in my "Bucket List" is to return to Vietnam, this time as a tourist, and walk the beaches of *Vung Tau*, and buy another pineapple, hopefully from that little girl – or her granddaughter - who brought me a small sample of God's bounty in a very troubled land. But reality sets back in rather quickly and I realize that she would be 50+, if she still survived. So Thank You, Pineapple Girl, for contribution to my sanity and a Thank You to Ray Funderburk, for all you did to bring the recognition to the Division. Thinking of these facts, I'm all the more grateful for such a variety of blessings, including my health, my family, my friends, and especially this great country in which I live. Now, if we can just keep the liberals from ruining it!

Cookies and the Church Ladies

RECEIVING MAIL WAS one of those events that helped us maintain some semblance of sanity – a small island of refuge in a sea of negative emotions. And it didn't matter if it was letter mail or a package of goodies – everything was welcome. And the usual infrequency of mail was compounded if you were hospitalized, based on the way that the Army processed your mail. Usually, your mail arrived at the battalion mail room and then it was sorted out by the mail clerk into company-designated sacks for next-day delivery out to the boonies. But for those poor souls confined to an in-country hospital, the mail went into another sack that eventually made its way up Highway 15 to the hospitals when the mail clerk was sufficiently motivated. Then the mail clerk at the hospital had to sort through the letters and packages, so see what might belong to the detailed list of temporary guests. So whatever mail you were supposed to receive last week was now another week late.

My latest stay at the 24th Evac Hospital was about to come to an end. For the previous nine days, I had been treated for "Fever of Unknown Origin," a medical term invented by the Army Medical folks and applied to any patient who didn't fit into any other injury/illness/disease chart. But FOUO, as it came to be noted on my medical records, had kicked my ass, providing such entertaining adventures as extremely high fever, bone-rattling chills, the dreaded 360's – alternating bouts of diarrhea and projectile vomiting – and an aching body that hurt from my hair roots to my toenails and every place in between. I have vague recollections of being covered by ice-cold towels that some beautiful nurse pulled from a large alcohol and ice-filled steel bowl ... well, maybe she wasn't beautiful, but she saved my life, a fact I realized years later after reading my medical records. "...fever 105.6 degrees....time 1737 hrs...." Even after I had evacuated my bowels of everything I had eaten in the last three years, my body was still rejecting anything taken orally, even small pieces of ice that I was encouraged to swallow to ward off dehydration. In the passing of time, which seemed like an eternity, and the compassion and skills of those caring nurses, frequent injections of penicillin and antibiotics, and the slight ability to retain some of the hospital's fine cuisine, I was finally rendered "fit to return to duty," and scheduled to be released back to the battalion. Despite the fact that my derriere strongly resembled and felt like a well-used pin cushion, I was heading back to the jungle.

Waiting for the driver from battalion to come find me, I was sitting on the edge of my hospital bed when a very overworked mail clerk from the hospital came into the ward, dragging two large mail sacks that were filled to capacity. Jokingly, I said to the clerk, "You can just drop that mail here!" The clerk quickly asked, "Are you Lieutenant Barnes?" My affirmative responses was quickly followed by a sound of relief, as the mail clerk handed me the ropes to the two mail sacks, "You got' em, sir!" And with that, he was gone. Opening one of the sacks, I noticed that there were dozens of packages, all addressed to me, and all with the same return address of my home church back in Texas.

Back at Camp Bearcat, I eventually boarded waiting helicopter with my web gear, my trusty CAR-15, and both sacks of US Mail, destined to be divided amongst my men when I got back to the Scouts. After the 20-minute flight back to the boonies, we landed near my command track. I motioned for a couple of my Scouts to carry the mail sacks back to my track because my bout with FOUO had drained me of any strength. But the excitement of getting this much mail was almost enough motivation to carry the heavy bags myself! Besides, I was happy to get back to my Scouts, my family.

So with the help of the crew of the BarneStormers – the name on my armored personnel carrier – I sorted out all the packages – 55 in all – more than enough to give one to every Scout, to both Combat Medics, and to my Artillery Forward Observer from the 4.2" Mortar Platoon. As we all quickly learned to our pleasant surprise, the cans - #3 size coffee cans – were filled with every conceivable variety of cookies known to those wonderful 'Scandawhovian' ladies at my church! Chocolate chip cookies, oatmeal cookies, sugar cookies, oatmeal and walnut cookies, coconut macaroons, ginger snaps, date and pecan fill delights – and others of delectable yet unknown ingredients – more than we should eat at one sitting! And in another stroke of benevolence, the cookies were packed in popped popcorn, which cushioned these absolutely delightful delicacies all the way from Texas. What a way to celebrate Christmas! Homemade cookies in an assortment and a variety that boggled the imagination, made with loving hands by caring ladies.

Three days later, after all of the cookies and the popcorn were consumed, I sent out a radio call to my Scouts, asking that at least one guy per track write a nice Thank You letter to the church ladies for their excellent gifts. Within a couple of days, I had a bundle to letters heading back to Austin, Texas, as my Scouts responded almost unanimously in gratitude.

Remembering how important and welcome were the "care packages" we received while serving in Vietnam, I resolved to duplicate this example of magnanimous giving by providing a plethora of brownies, home-made beef jerky and other goodies to our current warriors on various deployments. With my wife and me working together, we have sent many "care packages" to sons of various church members, as well as our two sons, my God son, and members of their respective commands. Thank you, Church Ladies, for your wonders example of giving and Thank You, current Warriors for protecting us graybeards!

The Stoic Bride and the Grunchfunker

ONE OF THE strangest missions the Scout Platoon ever received was guarding the Jungle Crusher, a one-of-a kind machine made by the LeTourneau Heavy Equipment Company
in Longview, Texas. This machine was used primarily to knock
down small trees and bamboo clumps around the various fire
bases, logistics areas and other permanent installations, oblit-
erating the vegetation behind which Charlie could hide. Its
hexagonally shaped wheel drums had concave sides, resulting in a cutting edge that ran the length of the 'wheel'; these
'wheels' on either side of the machine were rather water-tight,
giving the "Grunchfunker" – the name our Operations Officer
called it – the unique ability to navigate in the swamps of the
Rung Sat Secret Zone, a notorious VC hideout in our area of
operations, as well as in the jungle itself. The rear 'wheel,'
also hexagonally shaped, was the steering wheel for the machine. Permanently installed in the front was a push-bar constructed of 6" pipe welded in a triangular shape that pushed
the vegetation down so that the 'wheels' could crush it into
8' sections of pieces. Powering this mechanical wonder was a
large diesel-fueled generator that supplied power to the electrical motors for all wheels; sitting in front of the power supply was the operator's cabin, a small, 4' square cubicle with

minimum controls, surrounded by bullet-proof glass. The entire machine was controlled by a simple 'joy' stick and a few other levers and switches.

As with all machines, a certain amount of down-time had to be devoted to maintenance, and with the Grunchfunker, maintenance time seemed to be more than operational time. But this also gave us the opportunity to perform some much-needed maintenance on our own vehicles, some very over-worked and tired armored personnel carriers. These APC's had been used at Ft. Riley, Kansas, as the 9th Infantry Division was preparing for deployment to Vietnam, and had been shipped over with the Division; by the time that I became the Scout Platoon Leader, some of the 'tracks' had 15,000 miles on the odometer before the device broke, so the actual miles were impossible to determine. But the Scouts treated them with Tender Loving Care, knowing that this care may help save their lives someday, and it was this consummate professionalism that made the Scouts such legends within the Battalion and outside as well. This professionalism had been tested before, and would be tested again during the Tet Counter-Offensive and other significant battles. So while the Grunchfunker was being readied for more jungle crushing missions, the Scouts were quietly getting ready for the next test. Tet was coming.

Occasionally, an unannounced helicopter would land in our area and a curious general or colonel would ask about this apparition that sat in the middle of a clearing near the village of *Long Khanh*. Seen from the air, with some of its parts scattered about, it must have appeared to the casual observer to be something that needed close-up scrutiny. I had learned enough about the Grunchfunker to serve as the 'tour guide,' leaving the operator and maintenance personnel alone to continue working on their machine.

The residents of this nearby village were similarly curious about this mechanical monstrosity, but kept a respectful distance. *Long Khanh* was a neat and tidy little hamlet, populated by refugees from North Vietnam, who had fled the Communist tyranny before the partition in 1954, when the freedom of religion was eliminated in the North. Being staunch Roman Catholics, they had relocated to the South, where they could practice their faith without government interference, at least for the next few years, thanks mainly to the presence of American forces.

Our normal resupply cycle provided us with an occasional hot meal, with water, soda, beer, and daily mail, but one of the luxuries – ice – was rarely available. We longed for the opportunity to have a canteen full of really cold water, or to savor a really cold beer or soda, a luxury that seemed as distant as home. So some of my more enterprising Scouts took it upon themselves to overcome this logistical shortcoming by locating a reliable, if somewhat expensive source of ice. Another example of capitalism was soon to be established in *Long Khanh*! Cold beer almost made the daily C-rations palatable. So not only did Bill McCaskill and his close friend, SP4 Mike Velasco locate a reliable source of ice for the Scouts, they made friends with some of the local folks in the village. After several purchasing trips into the village, they invited me to accompany them on their daily purchases, when we met more of the villagers. In his own mixture of English, Vietnamese and Texas charm, McCaskill introduced me as the ranking member of our Platoon. Charming McCaskill even got us invited to a wedding that would happen in two days!

After dining on C-Rations and an occasional 'class-A' meal out of Mermite can for weeks on end, the prospect of real food, even if a bit different from what Mom would make, was a welcome invitation. As we were told, the wedding feast would take place in the covered pavilion adjacent to the church on the next afternoon, and McCaskill, Velasco and I were to be the honored guests. We wore the cleanest fatigues we could find, cleaned off as much of the mud from our boots as possible, and arrived at the wedding feast, clean-shaven and ready to dine on some exotic cuisine. I had learned long ago about eating in foreign places not to ask what was being served; if it didn't bite first, or crawl off the plate, it was probably edible. Even dog can be made to look quite tasty, and in fact, was as I learned later!

In the pavilion, the tables had been arranged in a square, and as we were seated, I realized that someone or several persons had spent a great deal of time preparing the enormous variety of food that awaited us. Everything from easily recognizable tomatoes and other fresh vegetables, - some raw and some cooked – with a panoply of sauces or gravies were being passed to each guest. Platters of different types of meat, cuts from different types of animals were also offered, but my plate was already overflowing. Out of the corner of my eye, I kept observing the new bride, and never saw a more stoic countenance in my entire life. I don't know if it was the local custom for the bride to just sit, silent and unsmiling, or whether she was seriously contemplating her new married life, but her emotion never changed. I never saw her look one way or another, never saw her take even one bite of food, and never saw her change facial expression. How she could maintain such stoicism in the midst of so much celebration, so much food, and so much happiness would be a mystery to me. Looking back now, I wonder if she and her new husband survived the war, and hope that they were able to find a new life in America, if they were part of the vast Freedom Flotilla that managed to escape the Communist tyranny.

It is still a mystery to me why some were taken from us,

while others, just feet away, escaped unscathed from the maelstrom of lead. Several months after the wedding feast, Mike was killed during an assault on a bunker complex. I mourn his death to this day, and doubtless will until it is my time to slip these surly bonds of earth. But something that isn't a mystery was the new friendship that developed between Bill McCaskill and me, a bond that has stood the test of time, and simply gets better with each passing year. And I Thank him for being such a magnificent ambassador of Texas in that small little Vietnamese village, and showing me how to find new friends and to enjoy exotic culinary experiences. I continue to treasure his friendship, as well as the pleasurable memories of the village that expressed such wonderful hospitality!

The Electrical Surprise

IF NOTHING ELSE, the United States Infantryman is the most resourceful person on earth! When given two bad meals out of either a box or a bag, he will produce a hidden plethora of condiments, such as bottle of Tabasco Sauce, A-1 Sauce, ketchup or some other variety of herbs and spices. For example, on my second tour in the Land of the Perpetual Fire-Power Demonstration, we subsisted primarily on C-Rations for all of our meals, three times per day, for a period usually not to exceed 35 days consecutively when we were in the jungle. As any Grunt from that period of time remembers, and probably wants to forget, at least some of the C-Rations all began to look and to taste alike, with the possible exceptions of Scrambled Eggs and Ham, Ham and Lima Beans (or Ham and something else we liked to call them, too profane to mention here!), the rare and endangered Pecan Roll and a few others. The one consistent thing about the 'meat' dishes in the C-Rations was a prevailing layer of grease or congealed fat, occupying about 1/3 of the can, and thick enough to be removed with a strong spoon or freshly-cut stick from the jungle. My little command group, consisting of my two radio-telephone operators (RTO), the company medic, the artillery forward observer and his RTO, all carried a variety of flavor enhancers or flavor distorters in our respective rucksacks, and somehow, these all helped to get us through another day of culinary water-boarding.

Resourcefulness was not necessarily confined to the dining room table, but extended to other needs. And the wooden ammunition boxes for 4.2" mortar rounds and 155mm rounds were always in demand for a variety of uses. Filled with dirt or mud, and stacked around more of our semi-permanent structures at the Battalion Tactical Operations Center, they provide some protection from incoming small arms and low-flying shrapnel. They also served as a stable place to rest your upside-down helmet, as it got used once again for a shaving basin, probably as designed by the genius who sold the pattern to the Army. These boxes were also used as a make-shift altar, on those Sundays when we were able to celebrate the Eucharist or The Lord's Supper. And on one extended operation, a stack of three boxes served as the 'barber's chair' when an enterprising NCO started his own barber shop on Operation Akron.

In the 2nd Battalion, 47th Infantry (Mechanized), we were exceptionally blessed to have a highly professional and dedicated 4.2" Mortar Platoon. At the time I recall, it was led by a 1LT David Bell, who was the consummate mortar man. Bell was the nominal leader, but the real work was done by a SFC Gordon Wong, a resident of Hawai'i and one of several "Pineapples" as the Islanders like to call themselves. Generally, the 4.2" Mortar Platoon was near the trail element in the Battalion order of march, with the Scouts usually leading the convoy on its new mission. When we pulled into a new location, the Scouts would make a complete circle around the new position, traveling in trail formation, until the perimeter was secured. If a line company was traveling with the battalion formation, they would move in next into their assigned sector of defense of the circle. The next group in the formation would be the Command Element and all their tracks, the personal APC's of both the Commander and the Battalion Operations Officer, and the M577's which linked together, would form the Tactical Operations Center. Naturally, they occupied much of the center of the circle, with a smaller sub-circle reserved for the 4.2" Mortar Platoon.

Usually, I rode in the lead track of the Scout Platoon, more out of vanity and a foolish disregard for landmines than out of bravery, as I hated getting dusty! During the dry season, the dust was not only thicker than a bad fog in New England, but impaired my ability to see what my other tracks, and the remainder of the convoy, were doing or not doing, so I rode up front. I also stayed a lot cleaner, again, which appealed to my enormous vanity. I also knew that there were times to get down and real dirty, and I had been there, done that, and knew that many more situations would present itself to get real nasty! But for now, I opted for the cleaner route!

To get a better look at the vehicles now pulling into position, I would stand on top of my track, and realize yet again how fortunate I was to be assigned to the Panther Battalion! The drivers carefully maintained the proper distance between tracks, all of the safety measures were being observed, and vehicles were moved into their assigned positions with a minimum of adjustment. As the 4.2" Mortar Platoon entered the large circle, the vehicles paused only momentarily as a lone mortarman dismounted his track, and with aiming stakes in hand, trotted out to start the process of "laying in the tubes." The Fire Direction Center (FDC) for the mortars was busily computing the data to relay to the guns, and before the last straggling vehicle closed the new location, the 4.2" Mortars were ready for a fire mission or ready to adjust their tubes. It was all a beautifully choreographed team effort, speaking volumes for the entire Platoon! Before I left on any mission with my Scouts, I always first coordinated with the 4.2″ Mortar Platoon, to see if I could stay within their firing fan and still accomplish my mission; they were the first folks I'd call when I needed indirect fire support.

Now that the guns were properly laid, the next major effort of the 4.2″ Mortar Platoon was to dig their own latrine hole, and using some of those wonderful wooden ammo boxes, create a very inviting and comfortable 'throne.' This new crapper was complete with a regular toilet seat, and just to the right of the throne was a stake about 4′ tall, with a brand new roll of toilet paper attached. And to make the facility almost complete, the toilet paper roll would be covered with a large empty tin can, naturally to keep the paper dry. But the crapper was not yet complete! The final 'touch' was accomplished rather surreptitiously by 1LT Bell and SFC Wong, who would extend some commo wire from the FDC to the crapper, not for a telephone, but as a "signal" device. The TA-312 field telephone was situated on the desk in the FDC, connected to the commo wire, which had its terminus in the toilet seat itself. Two nails had been driven into the toilet seat from the top, and extended all the way through the seat, and these nails were the terminal points for the commo wire. The circuitry was now complete!

Common sense, such as asking permission, should have played a role in some people's decision to use the 4.2″ Mortar Platoon's wonderful crapper. Where common sense prevailed, permission was promptly granted. Business was taken care of without incident. However, for those who were so presumptuous to think that they could avail themselves of this luxury, without helping to construct it, and without asking permission, an electrical surprise was awaiting them. Keeping an eye on the crapper, either SFC Wong or 1LT Bell would determine if permission had been granted, and if not, the TA-312 field telephone would be cranked up, and an electrical charge would be instantaneously transmitted to the miscreant's buttocks, as Forrest Gump so eloquently described! The response on the other end of the TA-312 was always predictable – a startled and verbal surprise, usually followed by a string of invectives that would make a sailor blush. If the guilty party was not through with business, the end result could be messy. The volume of raucous laughter emanating from the FDC was directly proportional to the surprise that the electrical surprise provoked. So Thank You, Dave Bell and Gordy Wong, for being great Mortar Men that you were, providing me with superb indirect firepower when I needed it, and for making the best and most luxurious latrines ever seen and used in the jungles of Vietnam!

My Lawn Chair

ONE OF THE good things about an armored personnel carrier is its ability to carry large quantities of ammunition, food, water, beer, bulk explosives, first aid supplies, various items of clothing, toiletries, and many other items that made a Grunt's life a little more bearable. This stark reality was brought home to me on my second tour in Vietnam when I had to honor of commanding a straight-leg infantry unit. Everything and anything that we needed had to be carried in a rucksack, or tied on to said rucksack, in some odd assortment of appendages. But that's a whole 'nuther group of stories!

When we were getting ready for another operation away from our basecamp, Camp Bearcat, my men would bring their duffel bags to the motor pool to be loaded onto the ACAV's. These duffel bags were crammed with what they might want or need for the next month or two, depending on the length of the operation. Somehow, I managed to find a wooden foot locker that fit in between what were the seats of the ACAV, but were now wooden frames that held the various caliber of ammunition we carried. Into my foot locker were two sets of clean uniforms, a minimalist version of a toiletry kit – no highly perfumed soap, no after shave, and no under-arm deodorant – but shaving stuff, toothbrush and toothpaste.

I highly discouraged any of my men from using any highly odorous stuff, as once we were in the jungle, I didn't want our position given away to the enemy by what was the cologne *d'jeur*. On the infrequent occasions when a scout dog was attached to our battalion, one thing the dog handler told us is that his dog would 'search' out the odors of the VC by the amount of garlic and other spices they used, and didn't want to confuse his dog with the American odors of 'Old Spice,' 'Aqua Velva,' or any other detractors.

My Scout Platoon had a very well-tuned and very functional *modis operandi* when it came to tactical movements, and actions to be taken in blocking positions, just as an example. After giving the order to stop, each track would be spaced properly to provide interlocking fires, pointed in the proper direction, and all personnel ready to receive any subsequent orders. One of the first things that were accomplished on each track was the creation of a sun shelter for the TC or track commander, or whoever was occupying the TC's hatch at the moment. Usually, a poncho liner was tied to the various antennas or any other point to provide shade form the scorching sun. On my track, this action was taken while the ramp was lowered to a horizontal position, supported by a 5 gallon oil can, followed by the placing of my bright orange folding lawn chair. I would sit on the ramp, either waiting the next order from the TOC, or trying to finish a letter to the family back home. This was my chair, one of the few luxuries I would allow myself, and a chair that the other four warriors on my track knew was for my butt only! If time permitted, another poncho liner would be erected over the ramp, making for a cooler waiting place for the next order or action.

Invariably, just about the time I was setting up shop with my lawn chair, Panther 6, the Battalion Commander would fly over in his helicopter, doubtless returning from an orders meeting at Division Headquarters. After he assumed command, we soon learned that LTC John Tower was much tougher than his 5'5" frame indicated. After gathering all the battalion officers in the Mess Hall, he announced in a no-nonsense voice, "Gentlemen, it's my job to find the Viet Cong, and it's your job to kill them! And believe me, I'll find them!" And so he did. He played bridge, volleyball, and war, all with the same 110% intensity of a man driven by his pursuit of winning at everything he did. In our rare times to play volleyball, he seemed able to jump above the net and smash the ball into the opponent's face with glee! At the bridge table, I found that being his bridge partner was as frightening as being his bridge opponent! And that lawn chair was like waving a red cape in front of the meanest bull in the pasture for him. He would immediately get on the radio after passing overhead, with a terse warning, "Panther Romeo 6, this is Panther 6. If I ever give you a mission, and you're not on the move in 5 minutes, I'm going to personally shove that orange chair up your ass!" If I could type this in Bostonian accent, it would sound exactly like LTC Tower, issuing his ultimatum! Needless to say, I never wanted to give him the opportunity to implant my beautiful chair where the light didn't shine, so keeping my Scouts in peak operating excellence was imperative.

But that didn't stop Panther 6 from trying to get the better of me! I now suspect that some of the little missions he sent us one were really his attempts to catch us unprepared so he could fulfill his promise to me! But as one of my Scouts related to me several years ago, 'the Scouts were a finely tuned fighting machine,' ready for any mission at any time. And this was true. Time and time again, the men of this platoon knew what order or hand and arm signal was coming next, almost the point of reading my mind. For example, we were on a small trail that broke out onto a dry shallow lakebed, called a "playa" in Spanish, and before I could signal to the trailing Scout sections to go into a line formation, the drivers started peeling off the center point, one section going right the next following to the left until the entire Platoon was on line. Then the fun started! One of my Section Sergeants, George "Hoss" Ottesen had spotted some wild hogs fleeing from a mud wallow, and asked to take one of them under fire. "Bring me some bacon," was my reply. So after a few well-placed shots of his .50 caliber machine gun, the Platoon stopped to let Slim do his magic with his ever-present knife. Apparently, Slim had had years of experience in gutting pigs, for in only a couple of minutes, the carcass of the pig, all properly field dressed, was tied to the trim vane on Hoss' track. While all of this hog butchery was taking place, the other Scout tracks were automatically maneuvered into a protective circle around us. No orders from me, just actions by some superb subordinate leaders that I had the privilege of commanding. Since we had worked the day before with an ARVN Ranger company stationed nearby, I figured they could make good use of some fresh pork!

With my command of "Saddle up," we were back into a line formation, heading away from the playa and towards the Ranger Company. Once there, I quickly dismounted and greeted the Ranger Company commander, "*Chou Dai Uy* Ngyuen!" After that greeting and exhausting my Vietnamese vocabulary, I reverted to 'pigeon' Vietnamese – a mixture of French, Texan, and GI - to convey the remainder of the reasons for our visit. "*Beau coup Chop Chop*," I said, pointing to the butchered hog, a statement that was enough of a translation to convey the message, and within 10 seconds, a small crowd of Vietnamese Rangers were untying the evening's meal to be.

Thinking back, I enjoyed that meal of fresh roasted pig as if it had been served at the finest barbeque joint in Texas, sitting in my beautiful orange lawn chair! And to make the memories even sweeter, I was given a brand new folding lawn chair, complete with silver colonel's insignia at the 2012 Regimental Reunion of the 47th Infantry! My good friend, literary mentor, and fellow raconteur John Gross, aka "Ranger John" or "The King," depending on the audience, had bought and decorated the chair, just for me. This time, many of my Scouts took turns, sitting in the Old Man's chair, which now graces the deck at my home, right next to my new hot tub. Thank You for the chair, John, and more importantly, for being the hero that you were, the man that you are, and the inspiration to others that you will always be.

But I would be remiss if I didn't mention a very special man in this story, LTC John E. Tower, aka "Panther 6," himself. Although we had a very special "love-hate" relationship, I still hold him as the paragon of Battalion Commanders of all I have served under. During the Tet Counter-Offensive, he was shot down <u>twice</u> while flying in a Command and Control helicopter during the most intense part of the battles! A lesser man would have been content to seek a safer vantage point in which to direct his respective fighting units, but not Panther 6, a man I now see as having a pair of really big *cajones*! And steel ones at that. And when I was seeking letters of endorsement to include in my application to law school, the one written by COL John E. Tower is still one of my most prized possessions. After his command time in Vietnam, he returned to the States, and served as part of the faculty at the United States Military Academy at West Point, New York, until his retirement. Living and working in the Washington D.C. area, he went jogging one day, and suffered a fatal heart attack after returning home. For making me a better person through your demands for excellence, I salute you Panther 6 and Thank You profusely for the leadership example you provided.

Lawless and the EM Club

THROUGHOUT THE LAST several decades of history and the United States Army, there has been a constant level of change regarding the proper and authorized headgear – or hats, as the civilians would call them – that would be allowed, required or suggested. Such names of hats as the KP hat, the Ridgeway, the beret, the baseball cap, the boonie hat, the patrol cap – and each one has its unique place in history or at least in the memories of those who wore them. (Even today, after a disastrous attempt to make everybody wear a beret, the Army has now sensibly backed off, and the tried and true patrol cap is now the utility headgear.) It was during the Clinton years, when morale was in the toilet, that the Command Sergeant Major of the Army, with the wimpy acquiescence of the Army Chief of Staff, decreed that a new headgear policy would certainly be the ticket to enhancing morale. Everyone would be ordered to wear a beret! Little did he know that the "beret is the thing" decision was met with derision and disgust, especially by that particular breed of Warriors who had to earn their berets, the Rangers, the Airborne troops, and the Special Forces, and now that distinction was to be diluted by some petty decision-maker.

During one of the odd stages of the war in Vietnam, some genius at an elevated staff position decreed that everyone would wear the baseball cap, not bothering to think about all the different folks fighting this war, especially those of us out in the boonies, as we liked to call our home away from home. For the uninitiated, the boonie hat had a floppy brim that circled the entire cap area, and was capable of being folded up and stuffed in a pants pocket with no discernible damage. It was ideally suited for use in the jungle, especially when out on ambushes or patrols. And only those of us who dwelt in the boonies were eligible or authorized to wear it. All of the other folks in the war wore the baseball cap, making the REMF's, as we loved to call them, very visible. For the uninitiated, "REMF" was a derisive term reserved for everybody who didn't go out and 'hump the boonies,' and was the abbreviation for 'Rear Echelon Mother F***er.' OK, you get the point. And it wasn't long after the official decree was posted about the baseball style hat as the sanctioned headgear that some enterprising Vietnamese tailor began to create what appeared to be a 'baseball cap' but was soon to be found as more comfortable than the Government Issue or GI version. And just as the boonie hat was worn in a countless variety of styles, shapes and configurations, so too did certain individuality arise with the shaping of the baseball hat. But irrespective of the molding and shaping, there was no mistake about the end product: it was still the *chapeau* of the REMF! One good thing about the baseball caps of that era is that no one was stupid enough to wear it backwards or sideways, as some morons have a tendency to do today.

My Scout Platoon was frequently given missions similar to that of our line companies, which meant that we were separated from the remainder of the battalion. On one such mission, we were given the mission of running convoy escort for engineer teams moving out on Highway 1, which turned northeast towards the Central part of Vietnam. At night, some of the platoon would perform 'road-runner' missions, designed to keep the highway open by preventing the Viet Cong from planting mines in or along the roads. (Just a little side-bar, but those things we now call "Improvised Explosive Devices" or "IED's" are the same thing we used to call "booby traps." Calling them an IED doesn't make them any more or any less destructive; it just shows how the more things change, the more they stay the same!) On the road-runner missions, we drive down an assigned stretch of highway for about 500 meters, stop, herring-bone – which means having the 'tracks' facing in 45 degree angles to the road, alternating with one 'track' aiming left, the next aiming right. Then I'd search for any suspicious activities with the Starlight scope, a classified piece of equipment that was really "high-tech" back then. With a very sophisticated battery/light amplification system inside, it would magnify any available light to the point that an almost daylight appearance would be available to the viewer. This device was the Army's answer to the claim that Charlie owned the night. Now that we had 'eyes in the dark,' his claim of nocturnal superiority began to wane. If no activity was noted, we would move forward another 500 meters, and repeat the process. Sometimes we got lucky, and spotted a new "dig" alongside the highway, and reported our find to the TOC. Fortunately, our area of operations was relatively quiet, but one night we did spot what I thought was going to be the trigger point for an ambush.

Since our internal radio intercom was inoperative, or just plain broke, I would not occupy the TC or Track Commander's hatch, but rode in the cargo area, standing up on the ammo boxes that replaced the seats. In place of my helmet, I would wear a set of earphones so I could monitor the Battalion command net and the Platoon net simultaneously and with a simple push of a button, I could communicate with either net. Any directions to either the acting TC or the driver was with hand and arm signals or a firm tug on the shirt of the TC.

The day before one particular road-runner mission, we had just received a crew-served Starlight scope to be mounted on our trusty "Ma-Deuce," the M2 .50 caliber heavy machine-gun that each track carried as its main armament. Before the road-runner mission, we took the track to a firing area on the berm of Bearcat, and after receiving permission to test-fire the weapon, validated the settings on the scope. With the patrol plan thoroughly explained and briefed back to me by my subordinate leaders, we set off shortly before dark for our assigned route. And as per Platoon SOP, as soon as we cleared the basecamp wire perimeter, all TC's automatically double-cocked the Ma Deuce, and placed a loose single round of .50 caliber ammo under the 'butterflies' of the trigger mechanism as a safety measure. Throughout several firefights, the Scouts had determined that it was quicker and safer to travel with the heavy machine-gun 'locked and loaded,' with that field expedient safety feature than to have to double-cock the weapon at the start of a firefight!

On the next leg of our road-runner mission, I was scanning the tree line as far as the Starlight would allow, hoping to discern the real from the imagined and knowing that sometimes the night can play tricks on the eyes. To demonstrate this reality, we were seated in this large auditorium at Ft. Benning, GA, as part of my Infantry Officers' Basic Course when I entered active duty as an officer. As the house lights were turned off, a single red light appeared in the middle of the stage, about three feet from the floor. The Infantry School Instructor then asked, "Which way is the light moving?" From the responses, it was determined that the light was moving left, right, up and down, but not all at the same time, and not all responses were from the same person. When the lights were turned back on, in the middle of the stage was a single chair and standard GI flashlight was taped to a side of the chair. The light had never moved, but without another point of reference, the light seemed to move of its own accord. From that lesson, we learned not to focus on the object we wanted to see, but to move the eyes to the right and left, and avoid staring directly at the target. Sure enough, using the hand-held Starlight scope, I discerned what appeared to be a person standing behind a tree, holding an RPG on his shoulder. I gently moved the Starlight scope back and forth across the 'target,' and came to the conclusion that my initial observation was correct. Gently, I pulled on "Red" Dodson's shirt, and motioned for him to use the crew-served Starlight scope and look in the direction I was pointing. "Red, can you see that dink behind the tree?" ('Dink' was the abbreviated form of '*dinky-dau*,' pigeon-Vietnamese for 'crazy.') "Yeah, there he is," replied Red. With the target confirmed, I sent out a quiet radio call to all Scout commanders: get ready for action, as I'm about to initiate contact. "Slip the .50 over to single-shot, and draw bead on that Dink," I ordered Red. "When you're ready, give me an up!" Ten seconds later, Red indicated that he was ready. "Fire!" With that, a single .50 caliber round ended the military career of a wannabee RPG shooter. We waited to see if there was any other participant in this poorly planned ambush, but apparently the others were frightened away by the noise and destructive power of the Ma Deuce. Thank you, Mr. Browning, for inventing this mighty weapon! The remainder of the patrol was uneventful, although still filled the tension of having driven through an area that could have been our death trap. We returned to *Long Binh* Post, where we would RON – Remain Over Night – until the next mission for the Scouts. But for now, to sleep, and perchance, to dream.

After catching a few hours of sleep, performing the

post-operation maintenance, and dining on some gourmet cuisine in the form of C-rations, Danny Lawless, my track driver and a few of his buddies walked over the local Enlisted Men's Club at *Long Binh*. At this time in the military, there were Officers' Clubs, NCO Clubs, and finally Enlisted Clubs, for the lower ranking troops. Generally, it was a small building, maybe with air conditioning, maybe a juke box, maybe a short-order grill, and invariably, cold beer. I strongly suspected that it was for the latter commodity that Lawless was going to the EM Club, since we had run out of ice, and when a cold beer just down the road, was a much better choice. But at least one warm beer was enough for Danny to set out on his quest for cooler climes and colder beer.

At least, that's the way it was supposed to work! Within 15 minutes of leaving for the EM Club, Lawless came stomping back to my track, and started to crank engine. "Do you mind if I ask where you're going," I asked, since I was still seated on the rear deck, composing a letter to my folks back home. "That sorry (insert your own brand of invective) club manager won't let us in 'cause we're not wearing baseball caps, and wouldn't let us in with our boonie hats! Now I'm goin' to drive my track <u>through</u> his Club not just over to it!" Lawless was my favorite Irishman, and he had a marvelous ability to physiologically morph into a much larger figure with every beer consumed. At this time, Lawless appeared to be at least six feet tall, weighing in at 185 pounds of lean muscle-mass, and more than ready to do some serious ass-whuppin'! In all actuality, Danny was a strapping 5.6" tall, and could only weigh 130# if somebody put wet sand into his pockets. His anger indicated that he had already consumed the height-adding phenomena although he hadn't even been into the Club, yet. "You aren't driving MY track anywhere, Lawless! Now let me finish writing this letter to my folks and I'll go have a chat with the Club Manager."

Ten minutes later, I was down at the EM Club, explaining some new facts of life to the Club Manager. He learned that my men didn't even own a baseball cap, would not be caught dead wearing a baseball cap, and that the boonie hat was good enough for wear in the jungles as well as in his Club. And I added that my Scouts could tear his Club apart with the slightest provocation, and that he needed to shit-can his silly rule about boonie hats. After nodding in total agreement with my rationale, the Scouts made a triumphant entry into the EM Club, and caused its profit margins to skyrocket. The last time I saw the EM Club in *Long Binh*, it was still standing. And from what I was told later, some of the REMF's were not standing, after having made a really stupid remark about my Scouts and their hats!

Thank you, Danny Lawless, for giving me an example of the indomitable Irish spirit. Later on, this same Irish spirit caused me to thoroughly re-examine my own heritage and re-connect with my ancestors. I now have a drawing of my own family coat of arms, linking me to the Emerald Isle!

Two Colors, Two Wars

WITH A SINGLE pronouncement back during the Korean War, the Armed Forces of the United States of America began the long-overdue process of integrating soldiers, airman, sailors and Marines into their respective branches. If former President Harry S Truman ever did anything worthwhile in his presidency, this decision was probably the best one. Someone much smarter and more informed than I said that the US military did more for bringing better race relations to America than any other institution, or force or law. In 1964, I was finishing up my 6-month initial training period after enlisting in the Texas Army National Guard stationed at Fort Hood, Texas, where I was assigned to the post airfield. 'Flight Operations Specialist' is what I had signed up for back in 1963, and expected to go to Keesler AFB to learn my trade after Basic Combat Training at Fort Polk, Louisiana. But the Army had better plans for me, and ordered me to Fort Hood instead of to Biloxi, Mississippi, where Keesler was located. But that worked out rather well for me, as I was dating a special girl at the time who lived in San Antonio, Texas, and driving there with a week-end pass was more practical than from Keesler!

Working at the airfield had certain attractions, but because of the irregular hours, I frequently missed the free meals offered by our mess hall. And living off an E-2's enormous salary didn't allow for many trips into nearby Killeen, Texas, for a meal. Back then, there were no fast-food businesses on any military base, no "Food Courts" in the PX, and very little ready-to-eat food in the small PX annexes. And one of my barrack's buddies, Edward Emanuel Rouse, had a similarly crazy work schedule, so he too frequently missed meals. But I had a car, a trusty VW Beetle, and could go buy a good meal on rare occasions. Rouse was sending almost all of his money back home in Georgia, to support his wife's college expenses. So one day, shortly after payday, and after missing yet another gourmet repast offered by our friendly Mess Sergeant, I suggested to Rouse that we go into town and have breakfast. The stunned silence and Rouse's countenance of pure unbelief that followed was slowly met by my realization that I had made a totally impossible request. Until now, it hadn't dawned on me that Rouse and I couldn't eat a meal together off-post. We had shared many meals together in the Mess Hall, but the 'outside world' was different. And I never realized how different until now. It was the summer of 1964, and the civil rights movement had finally coalesced into a political force, culminating in passage of the Civil Rights Act of 1964, which, among other things, forbade the segregation of cafés, restaurants, and other places catering to the public. No thanks to some professional Senatorial bigots like Al Gore, Sr., Robert Byrd, and Bill Clinton's mentor, J. William Fulbright, all Democrats and all who filibustered against it, the Civil Rights bill was signed into law, because of the eloquence, tenacity and common decency of men like Everett Dirksen, US Senator from Illinois, and other Republicans. Then it finally dawned on me why I was getting that incredulous look from Rouse! Naïve and immature, I hadn't realized that Edward E. Rouse just couldn't go into any business and expect to be served, only because of his skin color! "Come on, man, let's go, and I'll buy your breakfast! It's the law of the land now, and they can't make you sit in the back of the café, or the bus!" So off we went to desegregate the Highway 190 Café in Killeen. A couple of crusty old cowboys did give us a bit of a dirty look when we sat down at a table together, and soon a waitress brought us the obligatory glasses of water and menus. Nothing else happened, and we ate our meal in peace and quiet. I learned a good lesson in American culture that day, one that I would apply later on in my military career.

Almost three years later to the day, I was in Vietnam with the 2nd Battalion, 47th Infantry (Mechanized). Our unit was as fully integrated as it could, with Black officers, Black NCO's, and Black enlisted men. Of course, there were other races as well, including a Puerto Rican officer, Jose Torres, who looked like a very malnourished Pancho Villa, and whose antipathy towards the United States of America probably matched that of Pancho himself. We would mostly ignore his anti-American rants, but I did finally ask him if he was so anti-American then why didn't he just renounce his citizenship and find another place to live? Not surprisingly, he didn't have a ready answer, so we just ignored him that much more. Another more pronounced group was the Hawaiians, who self-effacingly referred to themselves as "Pineapples." But the positive side of the multi-racial organization is that we were basically "OD" or "olive drab," the unofficial color of everything the Army ever bought. We fought together as a unit, and did every other possible military activity without any racial rancor or distraction. In retrospect, I think that this is just one more reason why I have such abiding love and admiration for the veterans of the 2nd Battalion, and used them as a benchmark to evaluate every other unit to which I was assigned.

And that included by next assignment in Vietnam, leading

a rifle company in the 199th Light Infantry Brigade. Just before I arrived, the brigade commander has landed his helicopter in an area he thought had been cleared by the American units he was directing from the air. Fact of the matter is that area was still occupied by Charlie, and they proceeded to kill the commander on the spot. BG William Bond was well-liked by all the men who had the opportunity to meet him, but his personal involvement in this firefight cost him his life. There were too many instances where an officer way up the food chain became a micro-manager, relegating those commanders on the ground to just another over-paid radio operator. General Bond's replacement was BG Frederick Davison, the first Black general officer to ultimately command a US Army division.

But in 1970, some of the racial troubles in the States had found their way to Vietnam. In order to placate some of the demands of the Black soldiers, the Army allowed them to wear their hair in the "Afro" style, and the few guidelines about the size and shape of the Afro were soon ignored by the more militant Blacks. Discipline started to deteriorate, and the haircut guidelines were soon ignored, or only nominally enforced. Resentment among the White and Brown soldiers started to become apparent, when they saw the double-standard that was being applied. While some in the Black community argued that the 'Afro' was a legitimate expression of Black pride as it related to their ancestral history, that same history reveals that an 'Afro' type hairstyle is completely unknown in Africa at that time. It was strictly an American construct. While its distinct origins are unknown, it was probably created in some barber shop in the States, and the rage quickly spread to other Black communities and eventually overseas. One of the other "fashions" of the times was the elaborate 'dap' or greeting ritual that many Blacks adopted, modified, personalized and utilized as a way of greeting each other. I saw some White soldiers trying to emulate this process when meeting a Black soldier, only to be glared at with contempt and disdain. It was a Black thing. But if a Black didn't want to participate in the grand ritualistic greeting, then he became an "Oreo," Black on the outside, but White on the inside, as was explained to me by Specialist Cornelius. Before I assumed command of my rifle company, Cornelius had been an excellent soldier in the 2nd Platoon, and after recovering from wounds he received in a firefight, was assigned as the Company Armorer. As the armorer, he was responsible for repairing any of our weapons and any other duty that would enhance our combat effectiveness regarding our weapons. But Cornelius refused to participate in the 'dap' greetings, choosing instead to greet others with the more traditional handshake. He became an "Oreo."

At least when we were in the woods, which was the majority of the time, there were no racial problems, and we operated in the old ways of everybody being "OD." That suited me just fine. But when we returned to Brigade Main Base or BMB for short, the racial segregation and all its attendant evil was re-created by the self-imposed isolation and forced separateness by the Blacks. Peer pressure prevented many Blacks from associating with their fellow soldiers of a difference melanin measure. And most of my White and Brown soldiers refused to visit the EM Club for fear of being a victim of mob violence. Things were only going to get worse for the Army of the 70's, and I didn't want to be a part of that. So when the 199th Light Infantry Brigade was deployed back to the States, I was absolutely delighted to be assigned to the 2nd Civil Affairs Company, and attached to a MACV Advisory Team. I had witnessed two different colors and two different wars, and continue to this day to be grateful for my service with the 2nd Battalion, 47th Infantry, as a bright shining example of how things could be. I have no doubt that other Battalions in our Regiment experienced the same degree of professionalism, pride and ethnic harmony. Serving this Regiment as an Honorary Colonel has been one of the highlights of my life! In hindsight, I want to extend a hearty Thank You to Edward Emmanuel Rouse for his friendship, and for his bravery in helping to break the color barrier in Killeen, Texas!

The General's Chauffer

WHILE SERVING AT the 4th United States Army Headquarters at Ft. Sam Houston in San Antonio, Texas, I decided to apply for "Operation Bootstrap," the degree completion program for Army officers. I had not had a very stunningly successful academic career up to this point, but now realized that it was time to get serious if I was ever going to earn my degree. I experienced a mixed bag of emotions when my request was approved, and my orders finally arrived. After the typical name, rank, and horsepower info on the orders, the first paragraph read, "You are ordered to attend the University of Texas at Austin, for a period not to exceed 365 days, enroute to your next duty station, the Republic of Vietnam." This opportunity for 'free education' also meant another physical move for my family, from San Antonio, back to Austin, Texas. At least for my second tour in Vietnam, I'd go as a college-educated target!

So the process of defying the scholastic odds, prevailing anti-military attitude, and forgoing all semblances of social life began. In January, we moved back to Austin as I assumed the role of full-time student and part-time daddy and daddy-to-be, with child #2 expected sometime in September. For this wondrous opportunity to finish my undergraduate work, I would owe the Army two more years of my life, with the

Damocles' sword of a second tour as a combat leader in Vietnam looming over my head. I had already survived one tour, which include the infamous Tet Offensive, where my mortality was severely tested. But "orders is orders," as the saying goes, and the prospects of a college degree overshadowed the dangers down the road.

In 1969, attending any college or university as a veteran of the Vietnam War was the equivalent of wearing a target on your back for all the hippies and other human detritus to aim at. During my year at the University of Texas, I only had to wear my uniform on campus twice, and both time, felt more threatened than at any time in Vietnam! On the first occasion, I paid a courtesy call on the Professor of Military Science, the head of the ROTC Department, and the long walk across campus was met with some of the most hateful glares a human could conjure up. The other occasion was when I had to appear before a Regular Army Board at Fort Sam Houston, and didn't have time to change back into civilian clothes before my first class. Same degree of "welcome" by the resident liberals, hippies, and other malcontents. Later that same year, the nationwide protests and teach-ins took place, with all the usual suspects on the stage in their so typical regalia: long shaggy hair, hippie beads, filthy jeans, and peace symbols. Inflammatory and generally anti-American speech was the order of the day, and one of the "speakers" was a US Army Sergeant, in uniform, showing his neat row of three ribbons, meaning that he had been in Vietnam, and done nothing else. He was introduced to the crowd as an Army veteran of the "imperialist war" in Vietnam, and as a subject area expert because he had been there! As it turns out, he had been a supply clerk at *Long Binh*, knew about as much Vietnam history and culture as I know about Ethiopian mining operations, but was what the crowd was looking for, a veteran opposed to the war. Standing off to the side of the crowd, under a nice shade tree was a gentleman in a business suit, very dark glasses, and wearing a very no-nonsense facial expression. He couldn't have been more obvious if he had a sign around his neck that read: "FBI Agent!" So I approached him, showed him my military ID card, and asked in a matter of fact manner, "So, are you going to arrest him?" "Maybe" was his curt reply. Sure enough, as soon as our resident expert on Vietnam quit talking, Mr. Agent eased up and cuffed him before most folks knew what was happening! It seems that the Sergeant didn't know that participating in a political event while in uniform was a federal offense, or if he did know, he was too stupid to comply.

One day while eating a quick lunch in the Commons Area at the University, I happened to meet a graduate student from Taiwan, *Lo Dah Wen*, who was working on his Master's Degree in bio-chemistry. His family lived in Taipei, where his father, General *Lo Dah Pei*, was retired from the Nationalist Chinese (Taiwanese) Army, and was serving as a military-political advisor to President *Chiang Kai-shek*. When I told *Lo Dah Wen* that I was thinking about moving my family to Taiwan, so they would be closer to me on my tour of duty, he insisted that my family would live with his family. This situation prevailed until we could found suitable quarters, once they got settled into the routine of living in a completely foreign land. I had never heard of such hospitality, coming from a perfect stranger, but I eventually learned that this is common in Taiwan. I invited *Lo Dah Wen* to my home, where we had several very informative dinners, as I learned everything I could about Taiwan, and specifically Taipei. In fact, on one of those dinner meetings, we both experienced the lunar landing, gazing up at the moon that very special night. Back in the early '70's, Taiwan will still a very good friend and ally of the United States, and it would still be at least three years before President Richard Nixon would make his historic visit to Communist China, after the top-secret negotiations by Henry Kissinger, then Secretary of State, before Taiwan became an international pariah.

The prospect of a safe and secure living environment for my family, including brand-new baby daughter Holly, born in September, was very reassuring and comforting as I contemplated being back in the jungles of Vietnam. With airline tickets in hand, mine compliments of Uncle Sam, and my family's, compliments of scrimping and saving, off we went for San Francisco for a two-day vacation before I reported to the Oakland Army Terminal, right across the bay. Bidding my family goodbye, I was entrusting them to the crew of the Pan Am flight, the projected kindness and hospitality of a totally unknown and alien family, and the care of God.

After four months in command, and operating in a relatively secure area in Vietnam, I had the confidence to approach my boss with a request to make a quick trip to Taipei to see my family. My rifle company had seen little combat in the preceding six months, mainly due to the fact that the epochal events of the Tet Offensive and Tet Counter-Offensive. As I was to later learn, our Area of Operations had been almost 'sanitized' from all VC, as they had been used basically as cannon fodder by the North Vietnamese Army units that infiltrated to *Long Khanh* Province. These NVA too had mostly met the fate of their southern cousins, or had fled back to their sanctuaries in Cambodia.

After my R&R was approved, the S-1 – or Personnel - clerk drove me over to Camp Alpha, the staging area that processed all personnel going on R&R. The next morning, I boarded the bus for *Tan Son Nhut* Air Base which was adjacent to Saigon International Airport. Happily boarding the 727, I was offered a seat very near the cockpit; after all the other folks had been boarded, the cockpit cabin door opened, and a very gruff looking crewman motioned me over. "Do you want to ride up here with us?" He pointed me to a seat right behind the command pilot's seat, handed me a set of earphones with a microphone, adjusted the switches so I could communicate with the flight crew, and told the pilot we were ready to roll. I quickly strapped in as the rollout began; at threshold speed, I was delighted to see the scruffy neighborhoods surrounding *Tan Son Nhut* disappear beneath us. At approximately 6,500 feet altitude, the pilot flipped another switch, took his hands off the controls, and turned around to start a conversation with me. Sensing my terminal consternation, he assured me that the auto-pilot was working perfectly, and would soon vector us to the Manila approach at the *Nha Trang* vector point. Even back in the early 70's, air travel was safer than I could imagine!

Eventually we landed at Taipei International Airport, where I hired a taxi to take me to the General's house. Once we pulled into the walled compound, I saw a wonderful welcoming party awaiting me, a hodge-podge of people including my wife, my son Gregory, the General and his wife, the general's son and daughter-in-law, and off to the side, the general's chauffer and cook. Little Baby Holly was asleep, upstairs, recovering from the most pronounced case of chicken-pox ever witnessed in Taipei and points west. And so for the next four days, I basked in the opportunities to hold my ailing daughter Holly, to play with Gregory, to play with Gregory's mother, and to eat some of the best Chinese food I could ever imagine. Wow! Chinese food in Taipei, what a concept!

On one occasion, the General showed me a scrapbook of photographs of him and Mrs. Lo on their official visit to the United States. He had been wined and dined at various air force bases and Army posts as the U.S. strengthened its ties with the Nationalist government and sought to acquire a favorable response to the sale of some fighter aircraft to Taiwan. Justifiably so, the General was quite proud of his service to both the Nationalist government and to the U.S., so his genuine open-arm attitude towards my family was as natural as tomorrow morning's sunrise.

Part of the household at General *Lo's* residence was a retired Nationalist Army sergeant, who served as the chef for the entire family, and a retired captain, who functioned as the general's bodyguard, gardener and chauffer. I had been advised by my wife that the kitchen was the sole domain of the cook, and that trespassers were not welcome under any circumstances. Since I had no intention to piss off the cook or to cook any meals, I simply stood in the doorway of the kitchen, nodding my approval of his culinary skills while anticipated the next gourmet delight that he would produce. I did learn the Mandarin words for "great food" or "*ding hau*" as the natives would say, and made it a point to tell the cook after each meal! "*Ding hau!*"

Soon, way too soon, my R&R was coming to an end, and I needed to get back to the airport for my return to Vietnam. So it was back into my TW's – tropical worsted wool uniform, with all appropriate ribbons and such – as required by Army Regulation for R&R travelers. I requested that one of the maids – there were several that kept the house clean, did all the laundry, and helped with any other chores as needed – venture out to the side street to hail a taxicab for me. When the General heard of my request, he cancelled my instructions to the maid, and directed his chauffer to bring his car up to the main entrance of the house. The general's Cadillac was a 1958 model, immaculate in condition inside and out. Black, of course! As the car came to a halt, the driver hopped out, and immediately ran around to the passenger side; I was about to get into the front passenger seat when he opened the rear passenger side door, saluted with all the precision that would make a Drill Sergeant proud, and beckoned me in. Even years before "The Godfather's" famous line, I knew an offer I couldn't refuse! And off we went to the airport.

Arriving at Taipei International, there were already a half-dozen GI's at the airport, practicing that age old Army custom of "hurry up and wait." They too were dressed in their finest khakis, and from their ribbons and shiny Combat Infantryman's Badges, (CIB) I knew that I was looking at more of the beloved 'Grunts.' As the Cadillac came to a halt, again the driver leaped out, sprinted to the passenger rear door, and delivered another ultra-snappy salute! Happily, I returned his salute, and then heard the nearby Grunts comment on my arrival. "Holy shit, now that captain knows how to travel!" I stifled a big grin and headed inside the terminal for my ride back to The Land of the Live-Fire Exercise.

Thank You, General *Lo*, to you and to all of your spectacularly generous and kind family, for demonstrating the finest hospitality I could ever imagine, by welcoming my family into your household, and treating them as family. And Thank You, General *Lo's* chauffer, for the ride of a lifetime!

Free Drinks at the "O" Club!

IN MAY 1970, my rifle company was to be part of the invasion – or military incursion force, as the Brass wanted to call it – for the first legal trip into Cambodia. This incursion was Nixon's plan to wipe out the sanctuaries created there by the North Vietnamese, and had been off-limits to overt operations until the Nixonian Doctrine was enacted. Just minutes earlier, we had been quietly maneuvering through the jungle enroute to a suspected VC camp when the message came from the battalion TOC: "Move to the nearest pick-up zone ASAP, and wait for extraction by copters!"

It was only after we had arrived by at Brigade Main Base, better known as BMB that we were told to get ready invade Cambodia. Then the Rumor Monster arrived at my company area, and began his nefarious work, convincing some of my men that the enemy we were to encounter was 9 feet tall, ate raw meat and hand grenades for breakfast, and were meaner than the neighborhood junkyard dog. Men were strapping on LAW's, the Light Anti-tank Weapon, very useful against armor (which only arrived from North Vietnam much later), extra belts of ammo for the Pig, aka the M-60 machine gun, and extra M16 magazines for themselves.

Arriving at *Bien Hoa* Air Base, we were directed to a waiting C-130 aircraft. Instead of being fitted with the traditional nylon secants the interior of the airplane was stripped down to the floor and on it were skid pallets. My troops were instructed to board eight men at a time, were seated on the pallets, and a restraining strap pulled across the row. Then the next row of eight boarded, and the process continued until all my men were strapped in, a most inglorious and ignominious means of transport for my warriors. An airman with a two-day growth of beard and wearing a greasy T-shirt whose cleanliness mirrored the wearer asked me if I wanted to ride up front with the crew; figuring he was a loadmaster or some such title, I gladly accepted his offer, which was seconded by the young captain, who turned out to be the aircraft commander.

Climbing up the steps into the cockpit, I was told to sit behind the pilot in the jump seat, and then given a set of headphones. I looked around the cockpit to see who else was going to occupy the remaining two empty seats when the sloppy-looking airman sits down in the Navigator's seat. Slung over the back of his seat was uniform shirt, bearing the gold leaves of a major! Good thing I didn't go for an on-spot corrective action about his appearance, I thought to myself. Oh well, I had other things to worry about, much more important than some scruffy major.

The rollout and climb out of the C-130 were routine enough, and soon we were winging our way to the *Bu Dop* Special Forces camp on the Vietnam-Cambodia border. This Special Forces camp, like many others straddled some of the invasion routes that the North Vietnamese used in the attacks on Allied forces, and then reused when they fled back into their sanctuaries in Cambodia. Apparently, President Nixon had heard too many horror tales about this tactic, and a direct violation of Cambodian sovereignty. This unanswered challenge was a constant threat to the 'Vietnamization,' a gradual replacement of US forces with ARVN forces, that was to be the hallmark of GEN Creighton Abrams' strategic mission.

I had been briefed by our battalion commander that we would air assault into Cambodia from the Special Forces camp, into an area north of the so-called Parrot's Beak. Little did I realize at the time that my former unit of assignment, the 2nd Battalion 47th Infantry, would be leading the entire attack into Cambodia as part of a larger attacking force! But enroute, the weather started turning ugly, with large cumulus clouds signaling thunderstorms and rain. Lots of rain! The pilot also had to contend with certain mountains in the area as he made his initial approach. Major Scruffy was busily scanning his radar screen, and told me over the intercom, "See those white things on the screen? Those are mountains!" No wonder we were making such an adventurous approach to *Bu Dop*. Then another burst of wisdom from the navigator. "The runway is peena-prime. The last time we landed here, we slid half way down it before we stopped!" Peena-prime was a crude paving methodology, where oil or waste oil was mixed with water and some solvents, then sprayed on the packed earth as a form of ersatz pavement. The mixture was able to minimize erosion on the rounded edges of a road or runway, and did keep the dust to a minimum, for its good features. When it became wet, as it was now, it became almost as slippery as ice, which is not a good thing for landing aircraft.

Finally, the aircraft commander began a low-level approach to the runway, with lowered flaps, lowered landing gear, and a warning to all on board, including my ignominiously tethered troops in the cargo hold. Somewhat in jest, somewhat as serious as a train wreck, I suggested over the intercom something to the pilot that proved to be downright irresistible. "If you can turn this thing around, I'm buying drinks at the Club tonight!" Much to my surprise, and with only the slightest hesitation, the aircraft commander pulled back on the yoke, added more power, raised the flaps and the landing gear and responded, "That's the best idea I've heard all day! I don't like sliding down runways any more than anybody else!"

Thinking that we would be flown back to *Bien Hoa* Air Base, from which we departed a couple of hours earlier, the flight instead was diverted to *Tan Son Nhut*, the international airport at Saigon, which also was also another major hub of military traffic. For reasons known only to God and to the Loadmaster, an announcement came over the intercom, which was also transmitted to my warriors in the back: "We're going to be landing at *Tan Son Nhut*, instead of *Bien Hoa*! Remember, Saigon is 'Off Limits' to all US personnel!" He might as well have told them that drinking beer would cause loss of hair, or that a certain form of self-gratification would cause blindness. I could even hear the shouts of joy, all the way up in the cockpit!

After the C-130 landed and taxied up to the Passenger Terminal of the 8th Aerial Port Squadron, my company was unstrapped and off-loaded. I called for a company formation on the tarmac, adjacent to the passenger terminal, had the troops take off their backpacks and other gear, and ordered the platoon leaders to report to me. When they had gathered with me in front of the company formation, I instructed them to have all the gear lined up per platoon, leave one responsible person to guard the platoon's gear, and then follow me to the Officers' Club. I also told the platoon leaders that Saigon was off-limits, and that anybody caught there could be subject to a fine or court-martial. Since we might be leaving again at any time, I didn't want any delays in our pending out-of-country learning experience.

With my platoon leaders and artillery forward observer in hand, we set off for the Officers' Club, which proved to be only a few blocks away. Long ago, at least on my first tour of duty in Vietnam, I made a commitment to myself that I would never be in a situation where I was unarmed or best prepared for any situation I could imagine. Everywhere I went, except at Bearcat and *Dong Tam*, I carried my AR-15 and a Claymore bag – *sans* Claymore mine - full of magazines. Some folks liked the bandoleers for carrying magazines, but I found the bandoleer too difficult to extract the magazine from, and too much in the way if I had to assume the prone position, where-as the Claymore bag could just be flipped to the side. I was thusly attired when I paid a visit to the United States Embassy in Saigon, in the fall of 1967, to acquire a passport. Back then, a passport was needed if Bangkok was the R&R destination; my wife had made plans to meet me in Bangkok over the Christmas holiday period. I figured with the proposed 'holi-day truce', it would be a good time to leave my platoon. And opening the door on the Embassy, I was greeted by a rush of cold air, the likes of which I hadn't experienced in months, and a very uptight US Marine who was seated behind a desk at the entry. With a snappy salute, he said, "Sir, you can't bring a weapon in here!" The irony was not lost on me, as I tried to cool his sense of urgency, bordering on panic. "Relax, Marine – [how I really wanted to say 'Jarhead'] – I just want to get a passport." I was quickly informed that I would have to go around back, to the Consular Office, where I started the process.

So like my US Embassy experience, I was greeted by the same directive, this time uttered by a stunningly attractive Vietnamese lady at the Officers' Club. "You cran't bring gun here, *Dai Uy*, you check weapon here. I keep weapon for you!" I wasn't too crazy giving up my M-16 to anyone, but my interest in having a cold beer, a really cold beer, made me heed her advice or statement in fact, or one of the house rules, whatever. And waiting for us at a nearby table was our flight crew, already well into their second drink. They had already slipped out of their flight suits and into a sharp, clean uniform, and even the major had shaved and almost looked presentable in mixed company. Despite our lovely body aroma of *au d'jungle*, the Zoomies made room for us at their table, and I made good on my promise while approaching *Bu Dop*. Thank you, Zoomies, for having the good sense to eschew that landing at *Bu Dop*, and for all the other great things that the Air Force did for us in the Land of the Live-Fire Exercise.

Another Gift from the U.S. Air Force!

WITHIN TWO MONTHS of my assignment to the 2nd Battalion, 47th Infantry (Mechanized), I was offered a brand new, AR-15 to replace the standard M-16 which I had been issued earlier. In comparison, it was shorter, especially with the telescoping stock, and was a bit lighter. The heat guard around the barrel was different, as was the muzzle end, with no place to attach a bayonet. Good! Never did like that idea of getting that close to the enemy that I had to bayonet him! From what I was told, the introduction of this new model was for an evaluation to determine if the Army would adopt the AR-15 to replace the M-16. Apparently, nobody ever remembered to get my opinion of the new model, but I wholeheartedly approved of it. Now on my second tour in Vietnam, I was issued another M-16, and made my desires known, stating that I wish I had an AR-15 instead, but there was no AR-15 forthcoming. As Darrel Royal, long-time head football coach for the University of Texas used to say, "Dance with who brung you!" So I danced with my M-16, wishing all the while for an AR-15. Not too surprisingly, the civilian version of the AR-15 is one of the most popular weapons today, proudly wearing the "assault weapon" name given to it by the gun-control whiners and snivelers, and assorted bed-wetter's. But what the civilians can buy today bears no resemblance to the fully automatic weapon that I carried.

Back to the Land of the Live-Fire Exercise!

One of the "to-do" items for even a nominally good officer to accomplish soon after assuming command is to learn the names and backgrounds of his sub-ordinate leaders. I knew my platoon leaders, my artillery forward observer, and my two radio-telephone operators (RTO's), so now it was time to start learning others of my command who played an important role. There were all good men, causing me to reflect years later on that poignant and thought-provoking question, "Where do we get such men?" So I continued with my learning about my troops, without becoming emotionally attached to them to the point of losing objectivity and reason. But like me, my men were social creatures, and our bonding became something that no civilian or a non-combat environment person would ever comprehend. Maybe this is the most important reason why Vietnam Veterans band together frequently, just to be in the hallowed company of other warriors of that period, and just to bask in the sacred trust that held this special group of men together through the worst that humanity has to offer. Don't ask us to explain it to you, because if you haven't been there, there are no words to appropriately describe how we feel. Just accept us as we are, no better than you, just different in our own, unique way.

One troop in particular really stood out. He always seemed to be the point man – some say the most dangerous mission of an infantry unit – and never complained about it. On those occasions when I could accompany the 3rd Platoon, I could tell when he made "contact," as his weapon of choice was a .45 Thompson sub-machine gun, a holdover from World War II, a weapon that had been made famous by the super-heroes of the Rangers at *Pont du Hoc* at Normandy and many other places. The heavy and rapid-fire of the "thump-thump-thump" told me that he had opened up on another poor unsuspecting Cong. That sound was totally unlike the sound of the M-16. Like to sweet sounds of the .50 caliber heavy machine-gun that I had grown to love on my first tour, the sounds of the Thompson were just as melodic, in a morbidly macabre way, usually with the same result. The destructive nature of the Thompson was also a function of the weight of the bullets going down range, and this weight became a factor in how many "sticks" of ammo that the point man could carry. But because he was so well-respected and liked by all the other members of the 3rd Platoon, many of his buddies would carry a "stick" of .45 caliber ammo for him, and if necessary, would pass it up the line to him as he continued to lay down very effective fire.

So on the first available time to talk to this point man, I started asking him questions about his home, his education, his job before he enlisted or was drafted – all sorts of questions about his past, present, and future plans. For lack of a better name, we'll call him "Tony" although I can't recall either of his names. I do know that he was of Italian descent, and originally was from New Orleans, with that soft and very distinctive accent only N'orleans folks have. When I asked him what he did before he joined the Army, he replied, "I worked for da family!" I think that was all I needed to know, and was just grateful that he was an excellent point man and he liked his Thompson! Apparently, my complaining about my M-16 had reached all the way down to the troops, as he asked me when I was going to get an AR-15. "I guess when somebody gives me one!" was the only response I could think of at the moment.

Our C-130 had landed at *Tan Son Nhut* – the international airport at what was then known as Saigon – instead of returning to our point of origin, *Bien Hoa* Air Base. And after a night of visiting the numerous Military Police holding tanks and retrieving my wayward minions, we were ready to invade Cambodia again, or so I thought. We would be stuck at the 8th Aerial Port Squadron's comfortable tarmac until somebody way up the food chain remembered who we were, where we were, and where we should have been. After two very uncomfortable nights at Tan San Nhut, we were finally alerted that another C-130 would soon fly us up to *Song Be*, a basecamp for elements of the 1st Cavalry Division, where my company would be "OPCON" – Army jargon for "Under the Operational Control of"- for future operations. So our adventure into Cambodia was going to be postponed for yet another day or week or so. Who knew?

One thing I did know, or thought I knew, was that my Cajun point man was walking stiff-legged back to the company formation that I had called, all the way across an area where several USAF airplanes and helicopters were parked. I was going to tell them to be prepared to board an aircraft at 1330 hours, that we were going to *Song Be*, wherever the hell that was, and that we were going to be OPCON ['under the Operational Control of'] to the 1st Cav. To tell the truth, nobody seemed to care when we were leaving, where we were going, and what we were going to do when we got there! So after this brief announcement, and after I had dismissed the formation, Cajun Tony walks up to me in his stiff-legged fashion, and just as I was about to question him how he hurt his leg – probably in an attempt to get out of this Cambodian operation – he pulls an AR-15 out of his pants, and asks, "Is dis what you wanted, suh?" I had learned long ago never to ask an NCO where they got things, but that same rule didn't necessarily apply to enlisted men. "Where in the Sam Hill did you get this?" I asked, not really caring about the answer. "See that weird lookin' copter over dere?" Tony asked, pointing to a "Pronto," a helicopter used in fire and rescue operations. It had two opposing main rotor blades, that it could hover over an aircraft that was on fire, and the downdraft would enable crash rescue folks to get the pilot out. "It was just sittin' dere in da cockpit, and da door not latched, so I took it!" To Tony, that was perfectly logical: his commander had wanted an AR-15, Tony had the opportunity acquire one, so he took it - the opportunity and the AR-15! Fortunately, my company executive officer had just arrived from BMB, bringing the latest mail and a few more needed items. I gave him my old M-16 and told him to secure it back at BMB. So thank you USAF, for the 'loaner' of a new AR-15, and thank you Tony, for your gift as well.

Surviving Terminal Embarrassment

AFTER SEVERAL FITS and starts, our entry into Cambodia was finally happening. Initially, my rifle company started out at Bien Hoa Air Base, with a most inglorious and ignoble loading plan. We were driven to a waiting C-130 for the trip to Cambodia, where my soldiers were seated on a removable pallet, 8 men across, with a single safety strap securing all of them to the connecting ring on the floor. Then another group of 8 soldiers boarded the plane, to suffer the next round of indignities. As I watched the lack of proper planning that would have prevented piss-poor performance by the Air Force, I was asked by a grizzled looking airman in a greasy tee shirt if I wanted to ride up in the cockpit. A single seat seemed infinitely preferable to the mass seating arrangement that my men had to suffer. So after my men were all securely strapped in, I climbed the short staircase to the cockpit, where I was offered a seat behind the pilot. The greasy-tee-shirt guy turned out to be the ranking man on board, a major who was also the navigator! His fatigue shirt, which indicated his rank, hung sloppily on the back of his seat in front of a console of radar screens. It seemed like his disheveled shirt was going to be indicative of this entire flight.

Our take-off from Bien Hoa was uneventful, as was the

approach to Bu Dop Special Forces Camp. But when we were getting close to the Camp, the major hollered at me and said, "See all those white spots on the screen? Those are mountains, and I hope we can avoid them!" With a monsoon rainstorm beating against the windshield of the C-130, I began to appreciate the radar all the more. The co-pilot was walking around in the cockpit, trying to spot a reasonable approach to the landing strip, as we banked and turned to avoid the worst rain clouds and the mountains. Equipped with a set of headphones and a push-to-talk button, I could hear the entire conversation going on between all the crew members - pilot, co-pilot and navigator. Peering out the left side of the cockpit, I asked if we were going to land soon. The pilot answered, "Well, the last time we landed here, we slid half-way down the runway!" I certainly didn't want to learn a new definition to the descriptive phrase, "… slicker than owl snot…." The runway in this case was 'paved' in "peenaprime," a new word for me, meaning dirt covered by some oily goo and then nominally compacted down with a roller. I could easily visualize our plane and my company, sliding merrily along the runway to possible disaster, when I made an offer to the captain, the aircraft commander. "If you can get this baby turned around OK, I'm buying drinks at the Club tonight!" Yanking back on the yoke, causing the aircraft to start climbing up out of the rainclouds, the captain responded, "Yeah, I think we'll just head back home!"

Instead of landing back at Bien Hoa Air Base, we were diverted to Tan Son Nhut, the airbase at Saigon and its international airport. Why we were diverted are known only to God and some flight controller, and for the time being, neither one was telling. Naturally, there were no sleeping accommodations for us or dining facilities, or any other accoutrements for us international travelers, so we had to make do with what was available, only as infantrymen can do. A concrete parking ramp for aircraft became our communal bedroom, dayroom and gathering place. After being assured by the most senior US Air Force NCO I could find that our bivouac area was not going to be pre-empted by some itinerant C-130 or other ponderous aircraft, I ordered my platoon leaders to designate one guard per platoon, and then released the platoons to go find some place to eat. This was my first mistake of the evening. Less than 100' feet away on the other side of the security fence, the bright lights of Saigon and all her tawdriness beckoned my men like a moth heading for a flame. I had intended for the men to find a USAF dining facility – the Zoomies can't have a 'mess hall' – but it seemed that the majority of my men were yearning for something more cosmopolitan and exotic. It was going to be a long night.

With the weapons and rucksacks as secure as they were going to be, I told my platoon leaders and artillery observer to follow me to the Officers' Club, where I had a round of drinks to buy for our flight crew as reward for their absolute aeronautical genius in avoiding a slippery landing in favor of free booze. Thank goodness it didn't' take much to bribe our crew! And our flight crew was waiting for us, dressed in their tidy USAF khakis in stark contrast to our dirt-stained jungle fatigues. But to get to their table, I first had to surrender my M-16 to the hat-check girl at the front door of the Club, an act that made me feel quite vulnerable and naked. One round of drinks was quickly followed by several more, interspersed between a greasy burger and fries, followed by a Rusty Nail for dessert. Then it was off to play cowboy, as I had to start rounding up my errant troops from whatever Air Police Holding Tank they were occupying at the time. Most of my men had returned to the luxurious accommodations provided by the USAF, stringing hammocks between concrete posts, but a few absentees were to be expected. A friendly Air Police sergeant drove up, delivering the latest catch, and offered to drive me around to the various holding tanks to see if any of the current occupants were mine. By 0300 hours, all were present and accounted for, in varying stages of sobriety and injury.

The next morning, we were airborne again, me in possession of a new CAR-15 that one of my men had stolen out of a USAF helicopter, and my men in possession of varying degrees of hangovers. Destination this time: Song Be, home of the 3rd Brigade of the 1st Cav Division, to whom we would be OPCON (Operational Control) for the next five weeks. But instead of air assaulting into Cambodia as promised, we were detailed to provide perimeter guard along the airstrip for the next two weeks until somebody way up the food chain decided what to do with us. I was learning a new meaning for the term FUBAR.

Our long-awaited entrance into the Cambodian incursion, as it came to be called, began with an air assault into the smallest landing zone I had ever had the displeasure of visiting. In an area barely large enough for three Hueys to land, the local folks had practiced 'slash and burn' farming. Slash and burn is one of the most primitive of agricultural practices, where the locals cut down trees, leaving 3- foot stumps, burning logs, and planting around the ashes and stumps. But I wasn't there as an agricultural advisor. My rifle company was supposed to land there and then begin combat operations, searching for enemy cache sites. The first section of Hueys landed without incident, as I was notified by the leading platoon leader on the ground – "Cold LZ" - some of the nicest words I could have wanted to hear, with me and my command group scheduled to land in the second section.

As the third section was approaching the LZ, I remarked to Dave Reed, one of my radio operators, "He's coming in rather hot, isn't he?" The lead Huey of the third section had apparently misjudged his landing site, overshot it, and landed instead on a 3' tall stump, with the belly fuel tank immediately emptying its contents. Just 12 months before, I had worked as a volunteer at the Burn Ward of Brooke Army Medical Center, and had seen first-hand the horrible results of aircraft fires. All I could think of at the time was the flight crew stills trapped in the cockpit, stunned by the rough landing as my men jumped and stumbled out of the impaled Huey. I ran to the left side of the cockpit, opened the pilot's door, and managed to get the "chicken-plate," the armor side protector beside the pilot to the rear position. Knowing that an explosion might be imminent, I grabbed the pilot by the left shoulder and left wrist, pulled with the strength of a man driven by 15 gallons of adrenaline, and gave him the hardest pull I could muster. He hardly budged. Looking down at me with total disdain, he said, "Do you mind if I unbuckle first?" I could not have been more embarrassed if caught naked in the Queen's bedroom chambers.

As I slinked back to my command post, I was desperately hoping to become invisible, but instead, I radioed my battalion commander of what had happened, and suggested that he request a CH-47 Chinook helicopter to come rescue the perfectly salvageable Huey. As the next section of Hueys landed in my little world that was rapidly descending into chaos, one of the pilots - a 1LT Blue – I'll never forget his name - jumped out of the new arrivals, and ran over to the still-impaled Huey, performed the most cursory of pre-flights in recorded flight history, and declared, "Hell, this baby will fly!" With that, he jumped into the right front seat, fired up the Huey, and proceeded to literally pry the Huey off its landing stump. After several back and forth lurches, he was finally able to disengage from the stump, with JP-4, or whatever they call the fuel, still gushing from the wounded belly tank. Barely clearing the tree line where part of my company was securing the landing zone, the pilot made it back to the original staging area at Song Be, where I learned that he was immediately relieved of duty for being almost terminally stupid.

So if you see an old retired Army aviator, with left arm noticeably longer than his right, thank him for giving me that sterling moment of near-terminal embarrassment!

Dealing with Morons

AS THE MANPOWER pool for the draft in the Vietnam War started shrinking, the geniuses at the Puzzle Palace on the Potomac, known to others as The Pentagon - were struck by the Good Idea Fairy with the idiotic McNamara's "100,000 Plan." Mental and moral standards were cast aside in the interests of fielding more men for the stagnating war in Vietnam. These lower standards applied to both enlisted as well as to the officer ranks, resulting in soldiers totally unprepared for war, from the physical demands to mental agility required of proper decision-making. LT William Calley was a product of McNamara's warped thinking. We all remember the infamous deeds of Calley, and the dishonor he brought upon the U.S. Army and to America as well. One might venture a guess that 'political correctness' was born with the decision not to prosecute those officers above Calley such as Captain Medina and others. Personally had I been on Calley's court martial board, I would have voted to hang the little cretin, not give him house arrest for 6 months. The massacre at *My Lai* is yet another part of McNamara's legacy.

One such product of Ft. Benning's Officer Candidate School was ultimately sent to my rifle company as a replacement for one of my more senior first lieutenants. On first glance, he seemed fairly 'squared away' with his webgear all properly arranged per battalion SOP. He seemed intelligent enough and eager to learn how to be a successful lieutenant in the Army. I had asked 1LT Swanson to mentor him for a one-week period before leaving for his next assignment in a friendlier environment. But that event would have to wait for another two weeks.

When I assumed command of my rifle company, I was introduced to the three platoon leaders, the two radio-telephone operators, (RTO's), the company medic, the Artillery Forward Observer and his RTO, and finally the man who 'humped' the Two Niner Two, a portable antenna extension system that enabled radio communications in the jungle. This piece of equipment required the coupling of several aluminum tubes into one long pole and attaching an antenna at the top with a cable linking this system to the radio. This entire system was carried in a canvas bag measuring about two feet by five feet. It wasn't the worst burden for a Grunt to carry, but it was cumbersome and not easily transported through the triple-canopy jungle in which we operated.

After completing this little tour around the perimeter of the area being occupied by my company, I asked the lieutenant I was replacing about the man who carried the 292. "That's Weinegar, sir, Stephen Weinegar." Then I noted that Weinegar didn't seem to have a weapon nearby, and asked why. "That's Weinegar, sir, he doesn't get a weapon!" Incredulous, I asked, "You mean we're out here in 'Indian Country' he isn't allowed to have a weapon?" Under no circumstances I was told should Stephen Weinegar be allowed any weapons. The reason for the rather wild-eyed appearance that I experienced from Stephen Weinegar earlier simply underscored an earlier decision made by folks smarter than I not to permit Stephen Weinegar to be in possession of any weapons. But Weinegar would soon no longer be a concern of mine.

On the third day of our incursion into Cambodia, we were engaged in the first of several firefights, resulting in no friendly casualties, unknown enemy causalities, and one non-combat related evacuee. My new lieutenant, soon to be the new platoon leader for the 2nd Platoon, was ordered to board the next resupply copter with all of his worldly possessions, also ordered to never be in my sight again, and further ordered to report to the battalion executive officer. It seems that this young man, so promising at the initial impression stage, turned out to be a blithering dolt, falling on the ground and frothing at the mouth when the first incoming round was heard. Miraculously, he would recover his composure from what appeared to be a pseudo-epileptic seizure, and wipe the slobber off his chin the minute the firefight was over. This sorriest of excuses for a commissioned officer was so forgettable that I can't even remember his last name, even if I wanted to! In my report back to the battalion Executive Officer, I begged him to use every administrative vehicle possible to get this loser out of the Army. Fortunately, my command would not be further victimized by the idiocy of Robert S. McNamara. 1LT Swanson would have to continue as the 2nd Platoon Leader for another couple of weeks until a real lieutenant could be assigned.

After a typical 35-day operation in the jungle, we were allowed to hike to a pickup point. My company was met by several deuce-and-a-halfs that hauled us back to Brigade Main Base or BMB as the REMF's called it, for a very welcome 5-day stand-down. It would be time to eat a regular meal in the mess hall, instead of eating it out of a C-ration can, a time to get a long, way overdue warm water shower, a time to get a haircut, and more than enough time to drink several cold beers. On the day before returning to the jungle for yet another exercise in futility called 'combat operations,' I called a company formation to announce several items of importance. All of the platoon leaders announced, "All present!" except the 3ʳᵈ Platoon Leader, who stated, "All present, except Weinegar!" So before I dismissed the company, I ordered the 3ʳᵈ Platoon Leader, his platoon sergeant and the First Sergeant to make a thorough and complete search of the company area, and to report back to me within an hour. Within less than an hour, the platoon leader said that the entire company area, including all around the other company's areas and the battalion headquarters had been searched and no trace of Weinegar could be found. I instructed the First Sergeant to secure all of Weinegar's meager possessions, and then report him AWOL after five days, as per Battalion SOP. Something in my gut told me that Stephen Weinegar was long gone. There were no regrets on my part of his departure.

Ten days later, my rifle company was back in the jungle when a message came by radio that Weinegar had been reported as AWOL up the chain of command and to the local Military Police. I thought to myself, 'What type of a moron goes AWOL in Vietnam? Does this fool know anything about the geography?' With that report, I put Stephen Weinegar out of my mind for the next several months. Within that time, the brigade had been redeployed back to the States, and I had found a job as the Political Warfare/Psychological Warfare advisor to Advisory Team 28, where life was good. My luxurious lifestyle include a small refrigerator, purchased from the proceeds of selling some legitimate 'war trophies,' a real bed, compliments of the US Air Force – perhaps the subject of yet another story – an oscillating fan, and a private room near a shower with copious quantities of hot water for showering. This advisory compound even had a mess hall with two very good cooks, a source of decent rations, all adjacent to a well-stocked officers' club that had its very own air conditioning unit. Life was very good, but life for Stephen Weinegar was about to get a lot worse.

Arriving at my office in *Phu Cuong* City, I was enjoying my second cup of coffee when in walked a stranger, who identified himself as an Investigator with the Criminal Investigation Division (CID) of the Military Police. It seems that our boy Weinegar had been arrested in *Da Nang*, just before getting on the Freedom Bird heading home. As the CID guy explained, the authorities had charged Weinegar with 7 various counts or violations of the Uniformed Code of Military Justice, (UCMJ), with multiple specifications of each violation. "If convicted on all counts, how much time would Weinegar get," I asked the CID guy. "If convicted, and I don't see how he could escape any conviction, he would get a dishonorable discharge, forfeiture of all rank and privileges, plus twenty years at hard labor at Leavenworth," was his answer. The word 'Leavenworth' or the term 'The Big House' is synonymous with military prison, although Ft. Leavenworth is also home to some of the finest military learning establishments that exist, and not just the Disciplinary Barracks, as they are formally known.

With the ultimate incarceration of Stephen Weinegar, thus ended my direct involvement with one of the worst decision that ever oozed out of the Pentagon. The Army was now rid of Lieutenant What'sHisName, and Stephen Weinegar might be learning a new trade at The Big House. No Thanks to the ineptitude and gross incompetence of Robert Strange McNamara, I was almost saddled with two of the worst pieces of human flotsam that ever wore a US Army uniform, if ever so briefly. And if you'll allow me a bit of being judgmental, I think there is a very special place in Hell for McNamara and for Lyndon Baines Johnson as well. They both deserve it.

Fire in the Hole!

TWO DAYS AFTER my rifle company had found a sizeable weapons cache of SKS semi-automatic rifles, we stumbled upon another man-made cave that was dug into a rather steep hillside. As we were to learn later on, the hills of Cambodia were replete with these sites, a clear violation of Cambodian sovereignty, and one of the reasons why President Nixon ordered the Cambodian excursion. The North Vietnamese Army had used a large tree in front of the entrance to this hole to hide it from the air reconnaissance that was continually being flown in the area. But for us Grunts on the ground, the trail system leading up to the entrance was not that well-disguised or hidden. Now, the fun part started!

One of the first things we did on discovering any new cache site was to make a very brief but thorough reconnaissance of the area noting any particular land marks, and competing a sketch map to be sent back to headquarters on the first available helicopter. Simultaneously while this map was being prepared, the platoons were setting up a perimeter defense of the site, being especially alert for booby traps both high and low. After I felt secure that these two preliminary steps had been competed, I instructed the Search Team to begin its task of 'sanitizing' the cache site of booby traps.

Once this task of monumental importance was completed to the satisfaction of the platoon leader in charge, I instructed them to begin a more detailed search inside the cave, looking for any booby traps that might have been hidden amongst the boxes or crates that awaited further inspection. While not a usual practice of the North Vietnamese units that we had encountered earlier, I didn't want to make a fatal mistake that this site was also free of surprises that could prove fatal to the Search Team.

We were not ready to inventory the cave and to send the report that was being demanded by battalion headquarters on a repetitive 15-minute basis. It never ceased to amaze me that these numb-nuts at the Tactical Operations Center (TOC) were so oblivious to the element of security and that tasks in the jungle usually took much more time than they deemed necessary. To the repeated calls for an updated Situation Report (SITREP), my faithful and patient radio-telephone operator (RTO) would just tell them, "Nothing's changed from last report!" Just as tired as I was about these incessant demands for progress, I'm sure that battalion commander was getting hammered by brigade for updates as well. It seemed that the Cambodian Excursion had become very political, as I'm sure that MACV was being pressured by the White House to report something positive about the entire operation. My place in this word drama was very plain: I occupied the bottom of the pipeline, so the phrase, "Shit rolls downhill, and Friday's Pay Day," took on a new meaning for me! Pay Day would have to wait.

After three hours, we had a rather detailed list of the items we found in this cave. Box after box of the ChiCom 'potato-masher' style hand grenades, at least two dozen boxes of what initially appeared to be something resembling Kellogg's Corn Flakes, a very sophisticated piece of communications equipment, and 158 rounds of 120 mm mortar ammunition. The Lieutenant that led a team of engineers who arrived with the last resupply helicopter confirmed that the 'corn flakes' were a form of explosives, with a small demonstration away from the entrance. When I described the communications equipment that we found, the Operations Officer (S-3) insisted that I include this item on the first available helicopter bringing us ammo, food, and other supplies.

While the Engineer lieutenant was preparing the site for demolition, I wanted to recon the route from the cave entrance to the assembly area on the other side of the hill already occupied by most of my rifle company. It was important to me to find out how much time it would take for the Demolition Party, my command group and me to cover the route, as this time element would be a major factor in how much fuse cord to cut and insert into the first block of C-4 of the 'daisy-chain.' The route from the mouth of the cave to the assembly area was being secured by one platoon, while the other two platoons were guarding the assembly area. With this vital information in hand, I returned to check on the progress of our Engineer team. Everything that had been on the 'save and forward' list from battalion had been removed from the cave, and was being carried up the hill to the safe site. All that remained in the cave was soon going to be destroyed by the explosion of C-4, which in turn would cause the various munitions to detonate as well. At least, that was the plan.

Within the Engineers' Handbook is a wealth of information, charts, tables, that when properly read and applied, produces very predictable results. There are charts about the compression strength of concrete, of steel reinforced concrete, and of construction timbers. Other charts will precisely inform the reader of the length span that will support X amount of weight. More graphs will outline how much gravel will have to be compacted to form a reliable road or runway. But the chart I was looking for would show the length of fuse cord needed in terms of seconds of burn time. My route recon indicated that 9 minutes would be sufficient time to exit the cave, and have everybody safely inside the assembly area. The chart revealed that a precise number of inches of detonation cord would provide the time needed. Both the Engineer Lieutenant and I agreed on the length of the cord; I figured that two sets of eyeballs on the technical date was a good safety factor, as Mr. Explosion is not your friend. So the cord was cut, attached to a non-electric blasting cap, and inserted into a 1-pound block of C-4. This block was part of a complete detonation system, all linked together with detonation cord. I don't remember exactly how many 1-pound blocks of C-4 were used but it seemed that for each stack of five boxes of 120 mm mortar ammunition, there was a block of explosives. Just the simple math meant that there were about 30 blocks of C-4 just for the mortar rounds. By the time that all the other types of ammunition were linked together in the 'daisy-chain,' at least 75 pounds of C-4 was going to be used.

The fuse was lit, and an orderly exit from the cave commenced immediately. The security detail on the trail that led to the assembly area had been briefed by their platoon leader, and as we passed them by, they began to fall in behind us, forming the rear guard. I was nervously eyeing my GI watch, one of the most reliable timepieces I've ever owned, keeping track of the time for the pending explosion. All personnel were now in the assembly area as the final seconds ticked off. The standard warning of an impending explosion seemed pointless, but I yelled, "Fire in the Hole. Fire in the Hole!" Literally within less than 3 seconds of the estimated time of the blast, an enormous explosion erupted from the cave! The earth shook in violent defiance of man's attempt to alter the orbit of the earth as we began to witness the Law of Unintended Consequences at work yet again. Secondary explosions began as the cases of hand grenades were hurled hundreds of feet out of the mouth of the cave, a type of fireworks display that we had not anticipated or expected! If there were any enemy in the area of this second batch of explosions, they were soon covered by falling shrapnel and other debris from our handiwork.

After an appropriate length of time, ten minutes by my time keeping, we walked back to what was left of the cave site. The tree that had guarded the entrance was reduced to nothing more than a 20' tall trunk and that trunk had half its bark ripped off. The cave itself was totally reduced to a large indentation in the ground, a hole of freshly dug earth, and broken tree limbs and other jungle detritus. The Engineers had done an outstanding job prepping the site for destruction and that task was completed without injury or incident. My Thanks go out to the fine Engineer Team that conducted themselves with professionalism and great efficiency. And another day was marked off the 365-day calendar!

A Good Landing

WHEN I FIRST joined the Texas Army National Guard, my MOS – Military Occupational Specialty to the civilians – was a Flight Operations Specialist. Actually, it's been so long that I can't even remember the alpha-numeric of that MOS, and it's probably been changed since then anyway! My job included keeping the Flight Operations Center clean, posting the NOTAMS – special notices from the FAA to the pilots - keeping the coffee pot filled, and occasionally, helping a pilot in filing his flight plan. I had joined the Guard in an attempt to follow a high school friend into Officers' Candidate School, and ultimately into flight school, so we could go flying together. When I went to take my physical examination prior to leaving for Basic Combat Training, the doctor who had examined my eyes told me, "Soldier, looks like you're going to be a Grunt!" My faulty vision would preclude me from going to Flight School, and it was only much later – three years later, if that much! - was I to learn what a badge of distinction that title 'Grunt' would hold!

One particular Saturday while on duty at Ft. Hood, a lone aviator had checked out an O-1 or 'Birddog' aircraft to practice some 'touch and go' landings. As I recall, he was a particularly obnoxious major, eaten up with a severe case of

self-importance. My friend Gary Grimes was the sole operator in the control tower due to this being a weekend and that
there was so little demand for tower controls or instructions.
It was the common practice back then for the tower operator to notify the pilot that a 'touch and go' landing had been
recorded for him, so that the pilot could update his logbook
later after landing. The weather for this Saturday had some
rather gusty winds blowing out of the southeast, normal for
this time of year, but sometimes tricky for pilots to deal with.
On one approach, Major Haughty miscalculated the landing,
and bounced several times down the runway before actually
landing just long enough before adding power and climbing
out again. Forgetting that he had the 'mike's turned on, Gary
officiously asked, "And how many landings would you like
for me to record for you today?" Almost instantaneously, the
very pissed-off voice of Major Haughty came back over the
air saying, "Just one, G*d damnit!" Gary quickly turned off
all radios and any other electrical stuff, ran down the stairs,
locked the door to the tower, and raced to the Operations
Center where I was located. He was sitting there nonchalantly
sipping a cup of coffee when Major Personality stormed in,
demanding to know who was in the tower. "I don't have a
work schedule here, sir, so I don't know who's on duty," was
the lie to cover Gary's backside. He stormed back out, and we
just as quickly laughed ourselves silly over the entire episode!

There's an expression that I've heard about in aviation
circles that says 'any landing's a good landing if you can
walk away from it,' or words to that effect. As a passenger on
many air assaults in Vietnam, 'walking away' in all actuality
was 'running away' from the landing site as we sprinted for
the edge of the wooded area for concealment. We wanted
to avoid being included in any in-coming indirect fire from
Charlie if he decided to target the landing zone, as helicopters

were usually a big drawing card for mortar fire. But I digress.

By the time of my second tour of duty in Vietnam, I had accumulated several hours of 'stick' time in an OH-58 heli-copter, one of the smaller work-horses of US Army Aviation. Usually flying in very safe areas, the pilot would ask me if I wanted to 'have the stick,' aviation parlance for letting a nov-ice fly the copter. And despite the usual lack hand-eye-feet coordination at first, the pilot would invariably reassure me that "it's OK, I won't let you kill us!" So a new page was be-ing added to my dubious resume – an extremely amateurish helicopter pilot – as I worked one day closer to my DEROS.

This time, I had been 'loaned' the battalion's command and control copter to conduct a visual reconnaissance of an area for a possible future operation, as where we had been operating that had allegedly been sanitized of VC. Our battal-ion commander, The Old Man, was looking for new victories to proclaim and more headcount to report to higher head-quarters in his quest for 'bird colonel.' It seems that the Army had adopted a new criterion for selecting its future brigade commanders by choosing from those lieutenant colonels who had developed a more eloquent and convincing method of storytelling. And who was I to get in the way of somebody's upward promotion?

The jungle below didn't look any different from the hun-dreds of square kilometers of other triple-canopy jungle that I had either seen before from above, or trudged through on the ground. Trying to spot something in this triple-canopy that might have indicated some enemy activity was an exercise in futility, but I was enjoying the cooler temperatures and the feel of the helicopter controls in my hands. Then the pilot pointed to an area off to our right, and motioned for me to steer that way so he could get a better look at whatever he spotted. Swooping in a bit lower than my comfort zone allowed, I distinctly heard the 'crack' about the same time as the pilot lurched to his left, as the bullet penetrated his arm and the top of the copter. How it missed the main rotor blades is a question I have written down to ask God, when I get to Heaven!

I remember the pilot instinctively flipping the Emergency Frequency switch or whatever they call it, to sound an alert to any nearby aviators that we had an onboard emergency. Apparently there is a universally known and used frequency that is for emergency broadcasts only, and aviators monitor is along with the other two or three channels they have tuned in at the time. "Mayday, Mayday, this is Bronco 15, and we have taken fire, got a red light or two, and blood in the cockpit!" That message conveyed an encyclopedia of information that only aviators would understand, but I was too busy trying to keep the copter in a controlled descent that would not resemble a crash. I was being given great advice by my wounded pilot, and trying to apply it while thinking about a myriad of other things simultaneously, like how many bad guys were on the ground, did I have a round chambered in my CAR-15, how bad was my friend hurt, and where the f**k are we?

Answers to these and many other questions would have to wait, as I had more important matters at hand, namely how to steer this wounded helicopter to that small clearing off to the left side, and as close to the tree line as I could get it without whacking some trees in the process. The pilot was giving me instructions about what all to do, but I was only able to comprehend and apply about two-thirds of them, missing one of the most important ones of all: how to properly "flare" the main rotor in a timely manner that might enable us to walk away from the landing. Too late! By the time I had the collective pulled up into my left armpit, we had slammed rather hard in the small clearing, and with it, the attendant noise of breaking parts, an unstable main rotor making very strange noises, and a string of painful noises from my pilot, as the jolting had only served to exacerbate his wound. Once the main rotor quit turning, an eternity it seemed, I quickly unbuckled by harness and started working on the pilot's gear. I could tell by his facial color that he wasn't doing well, and I needed to get him out of the copter, into the shade, and then start applying whatever first aid I could with my limited resources and skills.

Another eternity was just recorded into my history by the time that I had dragged/carried the pilot from our wreckage to the edge of the clearing. I used the first aid packet on my webgear, contrary to what we had been taught in basic training, officer candidate school, infantry officers' basic course, and any other training about using the wounded person's bandages, because one might need one's later, but I didn't have time to search the wreckage and find his. The pilot was wearing one of those 'survival vests,' made with a multitude pockets, and searching for the right one was time neither of us had to waste. Whosoever bandage it was didn't matter – what really matter was that I got the bleeding stopped, got him to take a couple of drinks of water from my canteen, and continued to listen for what might be 'unfriendly' sounds. Due to some serious hearing nerve damage incurred during my first tour, hearing unfriendly sounds became more and more difficult, strain as I might. But a more beautiful sound soon became apparent, the distant "whump-whump-whump" of approaching helicopters! As soon as I had a visual line on them, I exited the tree-line and madly flailed my arms to give them my location, throwing a green smoke grenade for good measure and to give the pilot an indicator of wind direction. Although I didn't have any radio contact with the slicks, I just hoped that they would recognize a friendly on the ground. There were three 'slicks' all loaded with Grunts, and two Cobras flanking them; the slicks landed in the clearing while the Cobras began circling our position, in a lovely display of aerial combat power. As I learned later on, there were lots of salvageable parts of that helicopter!

A couple of Grunts ran over to our very fragile position, one of them being a medic, God's gift to the Infantry, and assessed the pilot's condition. Together with the Warriors, we carried the pilot to a waiting Huey, and were soon aloft enroute to the 24th Evacuation Hospital. The medic went back to the infantry unit, and I continued to apply pressure to the pilot's wound to minimize the bleeding. I recognized the 24th Evac Hospital from the air, having been a guest there many times before, and we were met by the ground folks who placed the pilot on a stretcher for a quick trip to the examining room and surgery. I finally found a friendly telephone operator who got a message back to the battalion's rear operations on Brigade Main Base, and then forwarded my message to the battalion TOC.

So once again, an abundance of God's Grace and Provident Mercy had been my unknowing companions on this fateful helicopter ride. And all too fleetingly, those heroes who slip in and out on one's life went without my thanks for all they did that one day. But many times, that is the very nature of heroism, those indescribable feats of bravery that go unnoticed and unheralded. To the helicopter pilots and air crew who brought us firepower, supplies, or rescue and aid, I extend my hand in eternal gratitude for the valor you continuously demonstrated.

A CONEX Container, Cameras, and Chaos

WHILE ASSIGNED TO the 3rd Battalion, 7th Infantry (The Cottonbalers), 199th Infantry Brigade, our battalion operations officer (S-3) presented himself as a self-anointed reincarnation of the Swamp Fox, Omar Bradley, and Genghis Khan, with all the personal charm of a coral snake. Imperious in his conduct, he barely had time for me a lowly captain serving as the Supply Officer (S-4) for the same battalion. Among his many talents, he was also a self-appointed expert on all matters photographic in nature, and being said expert, had invested multiple hundreds of dollars in an impressive assortment of cameras, lenses, tripods, filters, and other paraphernalia associated with the world of photography. All this gear was contained in several large camera bags and carried to the field Tactical Operations Center (TOC) for every operation the battalion conducted.

In one of his bursts of tactical prowess, the major decided that the battalion needed a "jump TOC" to be located about 20 kilometers away from our present site, to locate, fix and destroy an alleged Viet Cong unit. By this time, about 24 months after the massive Tet Offensive and the more important Tet

Counter-Offensive, there were virtually no VC units left in the Area of Operations, all of them having been annihilated by US forces in the Tet Counter-Offensive. The North Vietnamese Army units had used the local VC as cannon fodder in Tet, and what was left of the North Vietnamese Army units retreated back North to lick their substantial wounds. But I digress. The roads to the proposed TOC site were either non-existent or marginal at best, so the major made the decision to airlift all the supplies, equipment, and materiel to the new place via a CH-47 Chinook, the Army's workhorse medium lift helicopter.

Normally, a 'leg' infantry battalion TOC would have four main radios, with a couple of auxiliary receivers for command and control, operations and intelligence reporting, administration and logistics, and artillery fire support. And normally, one followed the Brigade's Security Procedures and loaded all sensitive equipment such as radios, the security paraphernalia that went with them, and any other items deemed by the commander as worth special handling. But this wasn't a normal operation, and it certainly wasn't a normal operations officer. He insisted that I bring a CONEX container, a 6'x'6'x6' steel box up near the TOC so all the radios and other supplies could be loaded. After I reminded him that the Brigade SOP required all sensitive items be loaded internally, meaning carried inside the helicopter, he reminded me who he was and who I was. So three out of the four radios, all the security codes and records, and all of his photographic gear were then carefully loaded into the CONEX, along with some tables, chairs, a small generator, two 5-gallon cans of gasoline, and any other item that would make the new TOC functional and operational. The major was busy coordinating the airlift for one of the line companies to be inserted into the new site to secure the area until the new TOC arrived.

I rode on the rough-terrain forklift as it carried the full

CONEX to our pickup zone to await the CH-47 that was to transport our precious cargo to the new TOC site. Knowing that a tornado of dust was about to happen when the CH-47 hovered over our CONEX, I reminded my supply sergeant to wear his goggles as he hooked the slings under the Chinook. As the Chinook was lifting off, I was already giving my pilot instructions to "Follow that bird," as I wanted to insure that the CONEX arrived at the proper place. (Side Bar: about two months before, another Chinook flying out of *Song Be*, a brigade base for the 3rd Brigade, 1st Cavalry Division, had an external load that started oscillating, ultimately causing the Chinook to be inverted, with the expected result of death to all on board.) Flying below and slightly to the right rear of the Chinook, I was watching the slings holding my precious cargo when one of the straps slipped for some reason, and the next thing I saw was the CONEX plummeting at terminal velocity towards Mother Earth. The CONEX hit a boulder about size of a railroad boxcar, ejecting generators, tables, chairs, and radios out into a fan-shaped pattern of total destruction. Hovering over the 'drop zone,' I could not discern a recognizable piece of camera equipment either. But the area was covered with pieces of paper which I immediately knew could only be the security code sheets that enabled the unit to communicate without the enemy hearing the actual transmission. That is, if the unit had any radios, which in our case we were almost fresh out!

Hardly containing myself, I radioed the SITREP (Situation Report) back to the one remaining radio at the old TOC location, and suggested that the Grunt company on the ground nearby move at all speed to the site of destruction to secure any SECRET material such as the security code sheets. I didn't have much control over my silent derisive laughter as I told the S-3 that his cameras etc. didn't survive any better than did his radios! But he had to ask! "What's the situation with my cameras?" Finally controlling myself, I said, "I think you'd better file an insurance claim for the entire batch, assuming you have insurance!" With that, I instructed my helicopter pilot to take us back to the original TOC site when I got a frantic call from the major. "Get back to BMB (Brigade Main Base) and bring back some replacement radios. We need them ASAP!" "Well, Duh!" I thought to myself, you used to have four radios to control the battalion, and now you're down to one, Major Brilliant, because of your completely stupid decision. So back to BMB we flew. But I knew that my next mission wasn't going to be easy, for the 199th Light Infantry Brigade, my major unit of assignment at the moment, had a motto of "Light, Swift, and Accurate." I was soon to find out what 'Light' really meant: they were 'light' of any replacements, floats, extras, or surplus when it came to major end items, like tactical radios. None, zip, zilch, nada, zero.

My introduction to grand larceny, to be practiced in much greater detail at my next assignment, was about to start. Back then, any vehicular mounted radio is supposed to be chained and padlocked to the vehicle – supposed to be being the operative condition. Cruising any parking lot that was unattended, I eventually found three radios, including one from the jeep of the Brigade Command Sergeant Major, and they quickly were added to my stash headed back out to the boonies. Now began the fun part, trying to find the least inebriated pilot who could be bribed to fly my loot back out to the field. Did I mention that it was dark by now, and that most helicopter pilots are either afraid of the dark, or are smart enough to know not to fly at night? I really think it was the latter!

With the promise of a bottle of Chivas Regal to be delivered upon a successful round-trip to the almost communication-less battalion, I finally secured the services of a semi-coherent and sober warrant officer, and our little nocturnal adventure began. Climbing to approximately 5,000 feet altitude, I could still see occasional green tracers, enemy fire directed towards us. So 45 minutes of flight time and what seemed like an eternity, we were nearing the new TOC. Unloading the recently purloined radios to the waiting S-3, he shouted over the rotor wash, "What took you so long?" Little did he realize just how close to meeting his Maker did he venture, for I was definitely in a homicidal state.

In retrospect, I should have confessed my theft to the Brigade Command Sergeant Major, as he would have then reported to his boss, the Brigade Commander, who doubtless would have relieved the major for incompetence and stupidity. The Brigade Command Sergeant Major would have gotten his radio returned, I would have extracted some degree of satisfaction, but may have also received a reprimand at least. But what I did learn is what type of officer I didn't want to become, so I thank the S-3 for his negative example.

The Travelling Typewriter

BEFORE I LEFT Austin, Texas, for my second tour in Vietnam, I paid a visit to the Managing Editor of the *Austin American-Statesman*, the local newspaper. Back in the Sixties, this newspaper was still a semi-respectable middle-of-the road news outlet, but has since fallen into the lower rankings of small-town liberal rags that basically are good for lining the bottom of the birdcage. I made a deal with Richard Seaman the Managing Editor that I would periodically send him articles, and if he published them, he would pay me the princely sum of $10 per article. As part of my undergraduate work at the University of Texas at Austin, I had to write numerous articles and papers for various courses, so a small, non-electrical typewriter became one of my most prized possessions. But on a captain's luxurious salary, that typewriter was a major purchase. Several years earlier, my brother had purchased an Olympia-brand typewriter, a product of fine German engineering and manufacturing, and it had served him well, so I decided that an Olympia would work for me too. While the advertising label said "Portable," the weight of the all-steel machine made lugging to and fro on campus a labor of writing, but my professors required that my course work be perfectly typewritten. Lugging it around Vietnam later would be both burdensome and rewarding.

Arriving back in Vietnam at *Bien Hoa* Air Base, all my baggage and personal items – including that wonderful typewriter - became quite a load to push through the line as we headed for the initial processing station. Adding in the expected heat and humidity, and I was soon wearing sweat-stained tropical worsteds, the reasonable substitute for the detested starched khakis. Loading all this paraphernalia to the Army bus for the ride to the 90th Replacement Detachment only added to the sweat factor, causing me to really question my sanity for lugging this heavy piece of machinery around.

As soon as I arrived at my initial duty assignment, the 5th Battalion, 12th Infantry, 199th Infantry Brigade, I quickly set up my typewriter and converted the long-hand version of my story about leaving the States, the long flight over the Pacific via Yokoda AB, Japan, for refueling, and the quiet nervousness of 200+ "Fresh" New Guys (some would call them FNG's with a different definition than 'fresh,') that were thinking their own private thoughts. For those of us who were returning to Vietnam, we had already moved beyond the heat and the humidity, and for us Grunts, the leeches, mosquitoes and other irritants that infested the jungles. And the VC or NVA, depending on the area of operations. After typing up my notes, reading it over several times and making some minor corrections, I mailed my first article to the newspaper for printing. Hopefully. Within less than three weeks, I received a copy of that article, printed exactly as I had submitted it, along with a $10 check. I mailed the check back to my folks in Texas, asking them to keep it for me until I needed a money order or some other form of currency. After several checks came my way via the Austin newspaper, I finally convinced them to simply mail it to my folks since I couldn't cash them anyway. My career as a bona fide 'war correspondent' was now launched!

Other articles followed, including one with an official U.S. Army photograph of one of the ammunition caches we found in Cambodia during the legal incursion. Each time I mailed an article back to the States, my folks would send a printed copy of it from the newspaper back home, and this copy would arrive about a week before my $10 check. And each article that I submitted was never edited or changed one iota, meaning either that I was an exceptionally gifted writer, or, more likely, the editorial staff at the Austin American-Statesman was exceptionally lazy. I have long suspected the latter. In either event, the infrequent checks accumulated to the point that I was able to buy myself a much needed "luxury," a small Hitachi refrigerator, which eventually served as a chilling repository for a bottle of Chivas Regal and Drambuie, requisite ingredients for my occasional 'Rusty Nail,' and a night stand for the most obligatory appliance, an oscillating fan. In addition to blowing warm air around, more importantly, the breeze from this fan kept the mosquitoes at bay thereby eliminating the requirement of slathering exposed body parts with the dreaded insect repellant. To this day, I detest having to spray on insect repellant to combat the mosquitoes, but at least some progress in the insect-repellant business has been made that makes the spray a bit more pleasant.

Carrying this heavy typewriter to my next duty assignment, the 2nd Civil Affairs Company, with further assignment to MACV Advisory Team 28 in *Binh Duong* Province, I was able to use this machine for a variety of felonious activities, including creating my own travel orders to go on leave to Taipei to see my family, or creating fallacious requisitions for necessary projects. Life with Team 28 was going to become a great adventure, both legally and illegally, and both inside and outside of Vietnam. And as the 'Psychological-Political Warfare' Advisor to the Senior Province advisor, I would learn to play in all of the four playgrounds, and to play well with others!

My first larcenous adventure was typing my own set of orders, authorizing me to take R&R in Taipei, to visit my family. I had previously checked with my boss, LTC Mullins, if it was OK with him if I took a few days off, and quickly got his approval. Then I talked to the Company Clerk, to tell him when to sign me out so that my travels would be official. When he asked about 'orders,' I told him that I had taken care of that locally! I can state without fear of contradiction that he never knew what I was talking about, could care less, and promptly forgot we ever had that conversation. Using an older set of orders that I used when I went on R&R legally, I simply copied the format word for word, except the effective date, and *viola* I was a 'legal' traveler again!

Today, I can state that my days of larceny and other high crimes are far behind me, and that I'm using a computer as my word processor instead of a typewriter! Looking back on the various and nefarious activities which are recorded here and in other vignettes, I can say that there was never any attempt to gain personal financially reward. "Stealing" the peanut mill, or the bridge-building materials or other projects were activities meant to help others, so the term "lateral-transfer" makes much more sense! Maybe this is just my quaint rationalization, as I didn't profit personally from any of these felonious activities, but genuinely tried to use my "talents" to help others less fortunate. Naturally, I'm grateful for the 'free pass' that was extended to me, and only hope that nobody had to pay for any of the missing merchandise! I'm also grateful for those fine German craftsmen for making such a useful machine as that typewriter!

After Duty Hours

WHEN I WAS first assigned to the Advisory Team in Phu Cuong, I met a CORDS employee who was on his last three weeks of assignment. Gary Langdon had served a 15-month tour and was more than ready to go home, after dealing with the quasi-Mandarin mindset of the Vietnamese civil service people. His frustration level apparently had long been met, and he knew that his effectiveness was rapidly approaching zero. As he explained to me, there seemed to be a lack of initiative on the parts of the local population when it came to making improvements without a stern directive from the upper management. The subconscious and prevailing mindset was almost fatalistic – "If Buddha wills it, it will get done"- seemed to be intellectual *modus operandi*, and getting people to "think outside the box" was much of a cultural or philosophical chasm to bridge. That negative attitude is the major tenet of Mahajana Buddhism as opposed to the Thervanda branch as practiced in Thailand and elsewhere. There were notable exceptions in any group, but generally these people did little thinking on an independent basis. But when given a direct order by the Province Chief, of course they would move Heaven and the *Cao Dai* Temple to get it done! Obedience to authority was unquestioned, but just don't ask them to be innovative!

Two weeks before Gary was to catch the Big Freedom Bird, he asked me to take over his extra-curricular activities as the resident school teacher for classes that took place in my office, after regular duty hours. He indicated that he had two classes, one for beginners and the other for a more advanced class of students. The students' ages varied from 9 to 39, with about every year in between.

Unlike most of my previous military assignments, my job as the Psychological Operations / Political Warfare Advisor to my Vietnamese counterpart did not entail a lot of extra duty time, so at the end of the normal duty day, there was little else to occupy my time. Of course, there was always the opportunity to and pleasure in visiting our little Officers' Club back at the Compound, but that soon grew old, listening to the non-combat types telling us how hard their jobs were and how many risks they were taking. On rare occasions, we would have touch football game on the grassy soccer field next to our compound, but being the less than athletic type, this too grew old. Unfortunately, I played one game too many, as we were in the middle of a rather feisty competition when I slipped on some rain-slickened grass, and severely sprained my right knee. This was the same knee that was damaged during the Tet Counter-Offensive, and the new injury just exacerbated the damage and attendant pain.

So once again, I was subjected to the varying degrees of quality of military medical practice. On my first tour, I saw the best the Army had to offer at the 24th Evac Hospital, and will be forever grateful to that crew that literally saved my life! But here at *Phu Loi*, the attending physician in the Emergency Room looked like he had been sampling either the results of a M-A-S-H distillery *a la* the great TV series, or else he had been hitting the medicine cabinet, as his eyes did not seem to focus too well. Without even X-raying my knee, he started the process of making a plaster cast that extended from my crouch to my ankle. Oh well, I gave him the benefit of a doubt, finally able to make it back to my hootch thanks to a pair of crutches. This mobility impairment meant that I would have to postpone my teaching chores until the cast came off, which wasn't too soon for me!

For the first two weeks, I managed to put up with the inconvenience of hobbling around on the crutches, having to explain to everybody I came in contact with about how the injury was sustained, trying to explain American football to Vietnamese, and as a final insult, trying to deal with the itches that were occurring under the cast in ever-increasing frequency. After straightening it out, an old metal coat hanger made a rather effective scratcher for those itches, despite the small clumps of cotton padding that was being removed with each scratch. But one night, I woke up feeling as if every bug and creepy-crawly had migrated into that cast, and the coat-hanger trick wasn't working. It was too late to drive to the aid station at *Phu Loi*, so I resorted to the next best thing: Cast Removal for Dummies. My K-Bar knife was kept in pristine condition, including a finely honed edge, and it would suffice as the tool of choice for the cast removal process; besides, it was the only tool available. But first, the proper anesthesia had to be applied, so I mixed myself a very large Rusty Nail from the chilled ingredients residing in my little refrigerator. I managed to get the entire cast cut off without the loss of a single drop of blood! Hobbling into the shower just down the sidewalk from my hootch, I thoroughly enjoyed the warm water and soap over the leg that hadn't seen or felt those items in too long of a period of time. The knee would just have to heal itself without a cast!

The next day, I was ready to start teaching my Vietnamese students. There were two different classes, one which met on Monday and Wednesday evenings, the other meeting on Tuesday and Thursday nights. The first class was really those at the beginning stage of learning English, while the Tuesday-Thursday group was much more advanced. In fact, several of these students were civilian employees of either the CORDS office, or of the Province government, people just wanting to know English in order to perform their respective jobs better.

Gary had provided some excellent source material from which I concocted somewhat of a lesson plan, and the learning process began. I made them an offer that they couldn't refuse: I would teach them as best I could, but they would have to teach me certain words in Vietnamese in return! Truth be known, I know that they learned much more English than I learned Vietnamese, but that was simply a factor in how eager they were to learn. As we were going through a particular sentence structure, it dawned on me just what a difficult language English is, and how much more difficult it was to teach, especially to people whose native tongue was so different. For a break in the drudgery of trying to explain yet another exception to yet another rule, I decided to tell them a little poetic ditty, as much for a diversion as for a teaching point. The ditty went like this:

A flea and a fly
Were trapped in a flue
And didn't know what to do.

"Let us flee," said the fly,
"Let us fly," said the flea,
So they fled
Through a flaw
In the flue.

I was trying to use this ditty to explain things like homonyms and how difficult it is to make all this 'stuff' sensible. But all I heard was, "Say it again, say it again!" in rather excited and amused voices! So, after repeating it two more times, I just decided to write in the blackboard for those that wanted to see it in print. As I recall, I didn't learn a single word in Vietnamese that night, but had a great time with my students. But every evening after normal duty hours, I would hop in my trusty jeep and head back into *Phu Cuong* City for classes, with my trusty CAR-15 across my lap, a round chambered, and a Claymore bag of additional magazines on the floor next to me. This routine was repeated for week after week, until it was time to be to leave Vietnam. It is with a perpetual sense of sadness that what English I taught my students may have been their death sentence after the North Vietnamese re-invaded the South for the third and final time. As part of their 'pacification and purification' process, those who had had any contact with the accursed American were the first to be either executed on the spot or sent to re-education' camps. Thousands died there, and those that managed to survive this ordeal began making plans to leave, by whatever means they could. Many thousands more died in this attempt to find freedom after their US allies deserted them to the ravages of Communism. I'm grateful for the opportunity I had to teach them to the best of my ability, all the while continually melancholy when thinking about their fate. I pray that many of them made it to America, so I can repay them as best I can.

Fishing in the Canal

AFTER SPENDING ABOUT six months of my second tour in Vietnam with the 199th Infantry Brigade, the eventual drawdown of US forces included that brigade's redeployment to the good ol' USA. For good reasons, they didn't choose me to carry the brigade's colors back to wherever they were going, which meant I would have to stay another six months in the Land of the Live Fire Exercise. My time with the brigade was not all that memorable, although I did lead a rifle company into Cambodia during the 1970 incursion. My company found many weapons and supply caches, including what had to be the largest bicycle parking lot in the world! Apparently every south-bound NVA soldier had pushed his bike down the Ho Chi Minh Trail with his allotted load of food, fuel, ammunition or whatever the hell his masters told him to strap on, and then park the bike at Grid Coordinate xxxxxxx, for a return trip to be determined later. When I reported this huge find to my higher headquarters, they decided that the bikes would be back-hauled by Chinook C-47 helicopters using an external sling net. So a Chinook would fly in, hover over the ground, a crewmember would shove the net out of the back, and the Chinook would fly off for some other mission. My men would straighten out the sling, pile as many bikes into the sling as it would hold, radio by the headquarters that a load was ready, and shortly, the Chinook would return, this time hovering above the bike load until we attached the loops of the sling over the hook on the belly cable. Off would go about 75 bikes to parts and places unknown. Then the process would be repeated, at least five more times, until somebody way up the food chain decided that every soldier, NCO and officer at that base camp had their very own personal transportation, and no more bikes were needed. But our next directive was to destroy all the remaining bicycles, by somehow rendering them useless to the enemy. Slitting the tires and bending as many wheels as we could, we complied as best we could without any resources being provided. Typical of how the military frequently operated back then: here's your mission, now go do it but I can't give you the tools you need in order to accomplish your mission!

Sometimes certain foods, like butter, were totally unavailable in either the Army's or the Navy's supply system. And when these long-lost commodities did arrive, there was usually an appropriate celebratory response. Our little Advisory Team housed on the outskirts of *Phu Cuong* City in *Binh Duong* Province, had a very easy life compared to other places and above-average meals were almost taken for granted. Being assigned to the Team was a welcome reward after serving as a rifle company commander for six months in an infantry brigade not known for its luxurious lifestyle. So when there was no butter to be had for our toast in the morning, we began to feel horribly deprived, with a concomitant amount of whining about our conditions.

Advisory Team 28 had a very eclectic population, with US Army Advisors, a contingent of US Navy Construction Battalion (CB's or SeaBees) folks, some US Air Force pilots who flew the Saigon rocket watch, and an assortment of

CORDS people. And as with most facilities by this time of the war, the behind-the-scenes people of Brown and Root, Inc. kept the generators running, the water flowing, and other life-sustaining activities. We later learned that Brown and Root was a gigantic construction company that existed solely or largely on government contracts with a large contribution going to Lyndon Baines Johnson for his political campaign fund and other purposes. Brown and Root later morphed into KBR, or Kellogg, Brown and Root, one of the major construction and utilities provider for the war in Iraq. The overpaid contractors of Vietnam had simply found another geographical location to practice their art of overcharging Uncle Sam yet again. Some things just stay the same.....

For the most part, life was good at our little home away from home. My office in town was in a colonial French style building, complete with stucco finish that once was white, tall ceilings of at least 12′ in height, a reasonable area of escape for the heat, and open areas for windows, allowing the variety of aromas ample entry. We could also see the local ladies who worked for the CORDS team, as they strolled by in their flowing *ao dais*, the traditional Vietnamese dress; they almost seemed to float, so graceful was their walk.

My counterpart was a very exceptional Vietnamese Major, Tran Phi Hai, who possessed a good sense of humor, who demonstrated initiative and resourcefulness in getting projects started and completed in the Province, and who loved his family of wife and son. *Tu Ta* – Vietnamese for major – also respected the time-honored tradition of taking a siesta after lunch, so I waited until the more appropriate time of 2 p.m. to call him and make my request. Earlier in the day, I received a call from my 'Sea Bee' buddy, informing me that he had obtained some butter through the mysterious Naval Supply System! And butter would be a major factor in the evening

FISHING IN THE CANAL ❯

meal we were planning; now all I had to do was bring the main ingredient – prawn – and the feasting would begin!

A small tidal canal ran through a part of *Phu Cuong* City, and with the tide in, a variety of seafood was there for the taking, assuming of course one had the proper fishing tackle. In this case, our fishing tackle consisted of *Tu Ta* Hai's son Truong, his dip net, and two concussion grenades. Two explosions later, *Tu Ta* Hai had all the fish he needed for his family's dinner, and I had eight prawns, enough to my Sea Bee buddy, LT Harris and myself. "Get the butter melted, and the water boiling, as I've got dinner!" was my radio transmission to Harris. I already knew that the beer would be cold, so no need to remind my Squid buddy!

Thinking back on this meal, it's amazing how good boiled prawn taste when dipped in freshly melted butter, accompanied by a freshly baked baguette and two cold beers, and a brother in arms who also knows some of the finer things in life! Thank you *Tu Ta* Hai for your contribution to this good memory, and my prayers are that you and your family escaped communism. And thanks, US Navy, for the butter!

A Bridge for Binh Mi Nam

IN VIETNAM, FUNDING for public works projects was in direct proportion to their respective distance from the Province
capital. So it was with the little hamlet of *Binh Mi Nam*, located at the far southern tip of the Province, about as far away
from the capital of *Binh Duong* Province, as one could get
and still be in the Province, and also occupied the lowest priority for any new or replacement projects, including bridges.
At one point in time in the dark days of pre-Tet, to venture
into *Binh Mi Nam* with less than a reinforced rifle company,
with attack helicopters orbiting nearby, was to invite certain
death or at least a substantial ass-whuppin'. But all that had
changed with the Tet Counter-Offensive. Despite the promises
of the North Vietnamese General Vo Nguyen Giap, the South
Vietnamese didn't rise up and overthrow their government,
nor did they take up arms against the American and other
Allied forces. For his own Machiavellian reasons, Giap used
the local Viet Cong basically as cannon fodder for his ill-con-
ceived operation, and the relative benign safety of the hamlet
was a stark testimony to his bad idea.

Through my Vietnamese counter-part, MAJ (or *Tu Ta*, as
they say in Vietnamese), I learned that a bridge in the hamlet
had been destroyed during the Tet Offensive. This bridge was

needed to access to the land on the other side, and the tidal canal was too deep to wade across. My friend, Paul Brown, the Agricultural Advisor for *Binh Duong* Province also knew of this missing bridge, and asked me if I could find some materiel in order to build a replacement. He and I drove down there for a visual reconnaissance and to get an assurance from the local folks that they would be willing to provide all the labor, if the materiel could be found. And since *Binh Mi Nam* was so far away from the Province capital, it wasn't included on the priority work list of projects for the Province Chief to consider. I suspect that the hamlet hadn't brought the acceptable amount of "administrative appreciation" funds to the Province Chief either, making their priority even lower! While Americans would either frown on this type of behavior or simply look the other way, a certain amount of "Tea Money" as it's called in many Southeast Asian countries, or *mordida* in many Latin American countries, or simply graft and corruption in America, is how things get done, and is a way of life. All you moral purists will just have to get over it. But I really believed that most Vietnamese were basically apolitical, and didn't give a pig's ear who was in power. All they wanted was to be left alone, to live their life with as little interference from government or anybody else for that matter. Not so startlingly, this is the attitude for about 98% of the world's population, I've come to learn. The one exception to this statistic is those detestable Muslim jihadists who have made life so miserable to so many millions. May they find their way to their Paradise as quickly as possible, and find out that those virgins are really frogs. I figured that if I could figure out a way to get a bridge built in *Binh Mi Nam*, the people would be happier, would have less time to plot against my visits which would become more frequent, and would keep the Province Senior Advisor off my case. A win-win-win situation was brewing!

Each advisory team was generally headed by a military officer in the rank of lieutenant colonel, or a civilian in the grade of GS-16. Subordinate to the senior province advisor was a team of combat-experienced officers that advised on combat operations, intelligence gathering, while the civilian advisors might help with military police matters, agriculture, or civic actions and projects. Normally, the province senior advisor reported directly to the MACV officer at their respective Corps, (or "corpse" as BHO would say!) and this report also went to CORDS (Civil Operations for Rural Development and Support). This often contradictory organization was responsible for the pacification of the countryside as part of the 'Vietnamization' process designed to phase out American military actions. I say 'contradictory' as a means of attesting to the fact that the State Department and the military were frequently at odds in how to win the war. It seems that the 'suits,' as the State Department is collectively known, didn't do such a fine job in Vietnam, and in subsequent wars such as in Iraq and Afghanistan. By the way, the selection process for picking Province Senior Advisors had to be steeped in alchemy, coupled with an extra potent batch of bat livers, cat entrails, and vampire piss. At least that must have been the creation process, which made us wonder all the more why we were stuck with this unreconstructed Nazi that headed up our Advisory Team. He walked like a gorilla in heat, and had a mindset that would have fit very well on the other side of the Atlantic about 40 years earlier. To further accentuate his bullet-shaped head, he elected to sport the completely shaved look. He inspired fear, not respect, and approached situations that normally required some tact and deportment with all the finesse of a runaway D-8 Caterpillar. Naturally, his relationship with the Province Chief bordered on the non-existent to tolerable disdain. But enough of him – I had a bridge to build!

Our advisory compound was located just a mile from *Phu Loi*, a huge basecamp that alternately housed elements of the 1st Infantry Division, the 25th Infantry Division, and other US Army elements, including both tactical and support units. As with every major basecamp, an Engineer unit was ever-present, either improving the defensive perimeter or building semi-permanent structures. And since supply accountability was something that seemed to be practiced only by Engineer units in the States, frequently there were piles of unused lumber, engineer stakes, pierced-steel planking, and other construction material lying around, just waiting for a larcenous captain. On one of my infrequent trips to *Phu Loi*, I had spotted some very useful items that were not in any supply yard, and their apparent disorder gave me the impression that they had just been abandoned in place. Note to self: this pile of stuff could be very useful in the future.

On my next trip to *Phu Loi*, I made a note on my clipboard just what building material was located where, in what quantity, and what security might be attached or nearby. A treasure trove revealed parts of an unconstructed Butler Building, a common pre-fabricated metal building, complete with nice steel girders and beams; other potential contributing sites had creosote timbers, pierced steel planking, and other necessary components of the bridge-to-be.

In 1970, one of the other features of *Phu Cuong* City, the capital of *Binh Duong* Province was the location of the ARVN Engineer School, commanded by a French-speaking Vietnamese colonel. *Tu Ta* Hai introduced me to him, and served as the interpreter. When I told him what type of building materials I could acquire, he began to sketch a bridge and the supporting structures in the sand, explaining it all to *Tu Ta* who tried to convey the idea to me. I explained what material I had seen and could probably 'acquire,' namely two pieces of a Butler building that would serve as girders, several 8" x 8" x 10' timbers that looked like very large railroad ties, and lots of pierced-steel planking (PSP). Several 10' sections of rebar would make the load complete. The design was in the hands of smarter men than me, which didn't take much. My earlier college scholastic attempts at engineering and architectural design were met with abject failure, scholastic probation, and a change in major to 'Government and Politics.'

Two days later, *TuTa* Hai and I were enroute to *Binh Mi Nam*, to reconnoiter the proposed bridge site again, and to recruit the active participation by the folks in the hamlet to support our project by contributing labor - rather <u>their</u> project! - since they had little else to offer. The very concept of building a bridge by hand, rather than using all the marvelous machinery America has produced – bulldozers, cranes, bucket loaders – was a miracle about to be made real for me. Then I remembered the stories about American infantry units and their actions in and around *Binh Mi Nam*. Too late. So with my trusty AR-15 that was acquired for me earlier, a claymore bag full of 18-round magazines, off we drove to the hamlet. *Tu Ta* was armed with a .45 caliber Model 1911, so I felt completely safe. Right.

Returning to my hootch in the Advisor compound, I began preparing my 'official' Requisition Form on my own trusty typewriter. Believe it or not, I had brought a 'portable' typewriter with me from the States, as I had made a commitment to the local newspaper back home that I would send them 'war stories.' While serving in a line unit, I had sent in six stories for publication, but now, I had a more important mission for the typewriter! With an impressive cover letter followed by a list of specific parts, I was prepared to begin my next larcenous adventure. Borrowing a 2 ½ ton truck (a Deuce and a half, as it's known) and a low-boy style trailer, my Vietnamese counterpart *Tu Ta* (Major) Tran Phi Hai and several of his enlisted men and I entered the base at *Phu Loi*, armed with my clipboard and 'Requisition Form.' Working as quickly as possible, we loaded as much bridge-making materiel as the truck and trailer would hold, and headed toward the exit gate which was guarded by an American MP. Theft of material from American bases had become a serious problem, so each vehicle had to be inspected to see that only authorized loads left the base. As we stopped at the gate, I quickly hopped out of the passenger side of my ¾ ton truck, and handed my clipboard to the surprised MP. "Specialist, I want you to check off each item on that Requisition Form to make sure we got everything! My colonel would really be pissed if I missed what he ordered!" The MP was so surprised that he immediately complied, duly noting each and every item on the truck and trailer. To compound his being co-opted, I ordered him to sign the Requisition Form, indicating that it was he who had 'inspected' my load and authorized my removal of the material from *Phu Loi*. Hopefully my criminal mind hadn't forgotten anything.

By the time we arrived in *Binh Me Nam*, half of the hamlet population was ready to help us unload the truck and trailer. Tomorrow, the construction would begin. And the next day, *Tu Ta* Hai, the Engineer colonel, Paul Brown and our respective drivers all converged on the hamlet to supervise the construction of the bridge. Work proceeded reasonably well, considering that there was no machinery or electrical tools available to move the massive girders, to cut the 8″ square creosote timbers to size, to drill holes in the timbers through which rebar would be threaded. All hand labor. Around noon, a small delegation of women from the hamlet brought an impressive variety of food for lunch, a tasty meat in a spicy sauce, steamed vegetables, bowls of sticky white rice, and fresh banana pieces covered in slightly sweet syrup. I made it a point never to ask what we were being served, if I couldn't recognize it. A week later, the bridge was completed, and I learned that my friend the Agricultural Advisor was already hatching his next nefarious plot, an even grander theft!

At the proposed construction site, we were met by what I perceived to be the hamlet chief, when up drove the Commander of the Engineer School, *Dai Ta* (full Colonel) Dao! He must have been really serious about helping, to make the long trip, all alone and unescorted. He repeated the sand-drawings to the hamlet chief, and by the nodding agreement, I presumed that the hand labor would be made available from both the ordinary citizens and the men of the local "Ruff-Puff" detachment that 'guarded' the hamlet. "Ruff-Puff" was the somewhat pejorative title the American had bestowed upon the Regional Protection forces that were actually recruited from within the hamlet they were to guard and defend, and had questionable skills in (1) using the weapons they had, (2) knowledge of how to discern the bad guys from the good guys, and (3) willingness to stick around in the event of an attack. While I was mentally questioning their ability to do their part, I realized that it was time for me to do mine!

The trip to *Binh Mi Nam* was uneventful, a variety of boredom that I was beginning to enjoy – the non-emotional rush of getting from Point A to Point B, without mines, ambushes, or sniper fire! *Tu Ta* and the local labor force were on hand as we arrived, and the unloading of the purloined PSP and other material was quickly achieved. The timbers that would eventually become the 'crib' upon which the girders would be placed were measured and cut with a two-man saw that mysteriously appeared from the hamlet. Holes were drilled into the timbers, again by hand, and the crib was beginning to take shape. The crib was constructed similar to a log-cabin with timbers placed at 90 degree angles, with the corners secured by a long piece of 'rebar' or reinforcing steel, the proper length being cut, again by hand. Once the cribs were built and inserted into the canal, another work crew began arriving with large rocks that were dumped into the crib, to stabilize it, and to keep it from floating away. Some of these rocks must have weighed at least 50 pounds, all hand-carried, all delivered personally by the rock crew. It was all an amazingly choreographed work-effort, seemingly self-directed, all for the common good.

By noon, much of the work for the first crib had been completed, and it was time for lunch. Long ago, at least when I first joined the Civil Affairs Team in *Phu Cuong*, that I would usually buy my interpreter lunch if we were out in the hinterlands on some project, with one caveat: I usually didn't want to know what we were eating, and don't describe the preparation process! With no McDonald's, Taco Bell, or Burger King outlets around, I was resigned to the fact that I would have to eat on the local economy, or starve until returning to the Advisor Compound. So I figured if it didn't crawl off the plate or bite me first, whatever my interpreter ordered would have to do! And the women of the hamlet had been hard at work, preparing the noon meal for all the workers, including the round-eyes who had brought them the bridge-building materials.

After the meal of "meat of unknown origins," some steamed vegetable greens, and the ubiquitous white rice, the work effort began anew. The sawing and drilling of the beams for the next crib was completed by the time I decided that it was time to head back to the relative safety of the advisor compound. But my dilapidated 'Jeep' had decided that it was not going to go another mile, much less the 25 miles back to the compound. My interpreter, Drung, tried desperately to get the Jeep running, all to no avail. Before he completely drained the battery in his attempts to start it, I decided to call our compound Operations Center, and tell them that I was going to RON (Remain Over Night) at the Ruff Puff compound, and to send the ¾ ton truck out the next day to tow us back. Suddenly, the bridge project didn't appear to be so altruistically necessary after all! But through an abundance of Grace that I had continually experienced, at least from the Tet Counter-Offensive of 1968 to this very day, I entrusted my safety to others who unbeknownst to them, were acting as Agents of God. In retrospect, I'm amazed that even nominal Buddhists, as many of my hosts were, could be used as Guardian Angels for this one Christian, proving yet again that God does work in mysterious ways! I guess that I need to be reminded of that on a daily basis.....

The hospitality of the Ruff Puff team was boundless! Magically, it seemed, cold beer appeared, along with another meal, a spare sleeping hammock and a relatively clean towel. I kept remembering all the tales of hostilities that emanated from this hamlet, and wondered if the Tet Offensive did indeed get all the bad guys. But I learned long ago, and still try to practice it today, that worrying solves no problems, and only serves to disrupt digestion, nerves, causes ulcers and sometimes gas, so worrying about the condition I was in would not help anything. And so to sleep, ...

Soon enough, the new day started, the bridge construction was basically completed, and I was able to return to the advisor compound none the worse for my stay in *Binh My Nam*. They had a new bridge – a very much-needed bridge – and I had another session of protection by my Guardian Angel. Thank you, good folks of *Binh Mi Nam* for your hospitality and hard work, and Thank You, Gracious Lord for your bountiful protection.

The Purloined Peanut Mill and other Larcenies

HAVING INITIATED MY career in grand larceny back at my former unit of assignment by stealing radios to replace some that had plunged to their deaths in a CONEX container, I was given another opportunity to refine my skills in my new unit of assignment, working on Advisory Team 28. My new title was 'Psychological Operations/Political Warfare Advisor, or the 'PsyWar guy' as I came to be known at the Advisor compound. And these newfound talents of mine were needed in *Binh Duong* Province, and had already succeeded with my bridge project in the hamlet of *Binh Me Nam*. Our province of responsibility, *Binh Duong* was a very blessed agricultural area, producing two rice harvests per year, along with a variety of row crops such as radishes, bok choy, garlic, onions, and peanuts. There was also a thriving pork production, to the point that the US government had contracted with a Taiwanese pig farmer to advise the local folks how to properly grow pigs. Taiwan, in case you don't know, in noted for its quality, trichinosis-free pork. If we could improve pork production, our farmers would be happier, and happy people don't usually participate in insurgencies! But growing and harvesting the peanuts also meant transporting the bulky crop to Saigon, where the peanuts were pressed and milled, the oil brought back in 5-gallon metal cans, and the peanut meal left behind as partial payment. Paul Brown knew that the peanut meal would make a great additive to the pig feed, further enhancing pork production, adding to the wealth of our farmers. And it just so happened that this same Agricultural Advisor knew that there was a disassembled peanut mill in a USAID (United States Agency for International Development, an agency within the US State Department) warehouse in Saigon, apparently just waiting for our larcenous actions! If only he had access to a 5-ton truck, a really good 'Requisition Form,' and a willing accomplice, that same peanut mill could be purloined and reassembled in *Phu Cuong* City, right in the middle of *Binh Duong* Province, and the peanut meal could stay at home where it belonged! Hmmmmmm. So we began our second collaborative act of grand larceny.

I explained to Paul how the process had worked so smoothly and successfully at *Phu Loi*. He had frequently visited the USAID warehouse, so another trip wouldn't raise suspicions. I would accompany him, and surreptitiously start making a list of crate numbers, and a parts list of the peanut mill. Then, back at my trusty typewriter again, I would prepare a cover letter to be 'signed' by the Province Chief, the parts, list of all requisite pieces of our little treasure, and the adventure would begin anew. But unlike my success at the MP gate at *Phu Loi*, the gate guard at the USAID warehouse was probably more professional and would require a copy of the requisition.

After explaining our venture to *Tu Ta* Hai, he agreed to loan us a 5-ton truck and some helpers to provide the labor to load the crates. So off we drove to Saigon, clipboard in hand, "Requisition Form' already signed with an illegible scrawl and a nervous sweat already starting to trickle down my back.

We were going for the big time stuff, not a petty load of bridge building material! Up until this point, I had never been to Ft. Leavenworth, even for official military business. I certainly didn't want an all-expense paid one-way ticket there. Too late, we were already pulling into the parking lot of the USAID warehouse. Paul explained that the peanut farmers of our province were counting on us! I was hooked.

Within fifteen minutes, all of the previously identified crates and boxes were neatly loaded into our vehicle of crime. As we neared the exit gate to the warehouse, I jumped out of the truck, just like my previous larceny, and quickly approached the gate guard. Repeating my previously successful con-job of the *Phu Loi* experience, I handed him my clipboard, and asked him to start checking off crate numbers as I called them out to him. "Make sure you mark them all off carefully. We don't want to miss anything!" It's truly amazing what an officious tone of voice can accomplish! Paul was standing in the middle of the truck, surrounded by the various boxes and crates, helping me call off the crate numbers, and probably sweating as much from the heat and humidity as from the tension. Grand larceny is grand larceny, and it applies equally well to civilian employees as well as us military guys! The gate guard was most cooperative, duly noting each and every crate. I thanked him for his diligence and attention to detail, pulled a carbon-copy of the list and Requisition Form off my clipboard, neatly folded them in half, and handed them to the gate guard. "Thanks for all your help!" I said as I boarded our truck for the ride home. All the way back to *Phu Cuong* City, I kept looking in the rear view mirror, hoping not to see some MP jeep behind us. From the sweat running down my back, I estimated that I lost at least a quart of water, literally sweating about the arresting officer that never showed up. As far as I know, the peanut mill is still in operation in *Binh Duong*

Province, still helping the farmers. One of my "Bucket List" items is to visit *Phu Cuong* City, and see if the peanut mill is still there!

Thank You, Paul Brown, for aiding and abetting a genuinely worthwhile larcenous adventure! And Thank you for caring enough about the farmers of *Binh Duong* Province to convince me to commit grand larceny! And Thanks that the statute of limitations has run its course so I can now confess the depth of my crimes!

Thank You, USAF!

WHEN I WAS assigned to the 2nd Civil Affairs Company, our little team stationed with Team 28, US Army Advisor Group had the most derelict vehicles I had ever encountered. Despite the herculean efforts of SSG Thompson, our ¼ ton vehicle, the infamous M151, the Army's replacement for the venerable Jeep, was in repair more often than it was in use. SSG Thompson would requisition the parts he thought would put our vehicle back in running order, only to find some other defect, failed part, or broken whatchamacallit would deem unusable again. When this vehicle wasn't running, we had to resort to driving our ¾ ton truck, a very reliable workhorse that we dubbed "*The Rough Rider*," as that was the only way to describe the effect of riding in this beast.

So it wasn't too surprising when SSG Thompson asked my permission to go to *Bien Hoa* Air Base, a major US facility about 25 miles away from our little home in *Binh Duong* Province for the stated purpose of finding some repair parts for our perpetually wounded vehicle, and maybe extend its life for yet another few months. I had some paperwork to do at the office, mainly the weekly reports to my headquarters of what we had accomplished, and what were our plans for the future. It was also on my schedule to visit the local prison, part of my job description, to see if the prison was up to the standards that the CORDS folks had set, mainly in the areas of sanitation, general cleanliness and other examples of humane treatment. At least from all outward appearances, the prison met and exceeded all these parameters. Most of the prisoners were either real or suspected Viet Cong, some of whom had been rounded up or captured during Operation Phoenix raids. Years later, back in the States, I read of the alleged incidents of physical torture and abuse by some US personnel involved in the Phoenix program or *Phuong Huong* as it was called by our Vietnamese counterparts. Thinking back on the one raid I participated in involving the Phoenix program, all I saw was very professional soldiers executing their duties with skill, efficiency and utmost precision. Due to the animus surrounding much of our entire mission in Vietnam, I'm not surprised that some story of utter brutality, torture, and mayhem would be written as part of the total denigration of our efforts, irrespective of the truth. We have only to look to our pompous and self-serving Secretary of State for verification of this previous statement. Fast-forwarding to our current war against terrorists, I realize that not much has changed, as some "journalists" are determined to vilify our warriors and their efforts every chance that presents itself. As part of my attempts to mentor young warriors-in-training at Fort Benning and other sites, or those who are already a bit more experienced, I remind them of the fact that the media is usually not to be trusted, and to handle them accordingly. I also remind them of a 'round-table' discussion, involving some military personnel and a few reporters, that was telecast on national television. The question posed by the moderator was, "If a reliable source told you that a VC ambush was located at position X, along a route being used by an American patrol, would you inform the Army commander of this ambush site?" To my utter disgust, the reporter said 'no,' as that might jeopardize his future relationship with the source! It was unbelievable to me that an American would place his foreign source above the lives of American soldiers! As I recall, it was Ed Bradley, of "60 Minutes" fame, who uttered this despicable rationale. My contempt for him knows no bounds.

But back in Vietnam, I was still awaiting the return of my sergeant and our tired old vehicle. Perhaps to a fault, I was concerned about my NCO, as I cared for all the fine soldiers who had ever been under my command, and less concerned about my vehicle, but knowing its basic unworthiness caused my concern for SSG Thompson to double. It was getting close to the time to close the office and head back to our home away from home, the Team 28 Advisor Compound, when SSG Thomson drove up in what looked like a brand new, shiny M151! The USA numbers and other identification were a brilliant white, while the OD of the remainder of the 'jeep' was as shiny as a new dime. And then the distinct aroma of fresh paint wafted to my nostrils! Without asking any other question, I simply asked SSG Thompson, "How much is this going to cost me?" Without batting an eye, he replied, "Two cartoons of Salems, and three cases of beer." This little purchase by SSG Thompson had maxed out his MACV Ration Card, which allowed US personnel to buy a limited amount of items from our PX system. Beer and cigarettes were hot items on the black market, hence the limited amount of purchases. SSG Thompson had used his monthly allotment to pay for the repainting and lettering on our new "wheels," which were also festooned with brand new fake leather seat covers! My good sergeant was even clever enough to locate the new log book.

As the story was relayed to me later, SSG Thompson had driven to *Bien Hoa* Air Base and attempted to barter some captured VC weapons for some spare parts for our near-terminal jeep. Unable to get a good deal, he stopped next to the PX at *Bien Hoa*, one of the largest in Vietnam at the time, and a popular stopping place for US personnel. Thompson used his MACV Ration Card to the maximum, buying some beer and cigarettes that might find its way back to the little NCO Club on the grounds of our compound. At least that was his intent! The parking lot was full of military vehicles, mainly jeeps, and an occasional deuce and a half. Apparently the larcenous behavior of his commanding officer had rubbed off on SSG Thompson, so the first jeep he found that was unlocked became an object of his affection! Quickly, he transferred his recent purchases and our old log book to the new vehicle and waiting for the right moment, made his way to the Main Gate. The MP at the gate gave him only a cursory glance and waved him on, with the next stop being a local auto repair and body paint shop.

So the nefarious trip contained an explanation as to why my good sergeant was so late in returning to the office, but after I had seen the results of his enterprising and felonious ways, I certainly forgave him. Our old jeep was reported stolen to the proper authorities, who probably threw our report into the circular file as soon as we hung up the phone! By this time in the war, people were just marching in place, not wanting to stir up anything that might delay their departure from what had been their own private little hell. And fortunately for us, nobody came snooping around either our office in *Phu Cuong* City or at the Advisors' Compound. The last time I saw our gift from the USAF was when it dropped me off at *Tan Son Nhut* for my last flight out of Vietnam. My Thank You goes to SSG Thompson, my hard-working if somewhat dishonest sergeant, and to the sloppy security of the United States Air Force!

The Indestructible Porcelain Temple Dog

AFTER SERVING AS an Infantry Company Commander on my second tour in RVN, my assignment as a Civil Affairs Platoon Leader seemed somewhat of a demotion, until I learned that the Civil Affairs Company Commander was actually a lieutenant colonel! So being a platoon leader wasn't so bad after all, especially considering all the fun chores that lay ahead of me. For the remaining 6 months, I would to able and willing to commit several acts of grand larceny, forgery, receiving stolen property, all the while being able to sleep in a real bed, able to take daily warm water showers, and willing to enjoy a frequent Rusty Nail at bedtime. Life in the Advisors' Compound was going to be good.

"Winning the Hearts and Minds of the Vietnamese People" had been a public relations/civic action slogan so long and only worked if both parties were actively committed to making it work. Most of the infantrymen I knew, especially those at the higher ranks, viewed the slogan with sardonic cynicism such as, "If you grab them by the balls, their hearts and minds will follow." That statement certainly is true, up until the point that when you let go of their balls, then they just might revert to being a Viet Cong and turn around and kill you. Officially, my job as the Psychological/Political Warfare Advisor to the Province Political Warfare officer required me to take a totally different approach to the remaining Viet Cong in the area. What made my job so much easier is that most of the VC had been killed months earlier during the Tet Offensive, which turned out to be a debacle of major proportions, according to General Vo Nyguen Giap, HMFIC of the North Vietnamese Army. In a different part of the country on my first tour of duty, I had been a player in that slaughter of the enemy. It wasn't personal, it was business, and my business was made much easier by an incredible group of men that I had the honor of serving with. The officers and men of the 2nd Battalion, 47th Infantry (Mechanized) taught me so much about life, combat operations, surviving in base camps, and other inscrutable lessons that I can never thank them enough. Now, my current job was also made easier by my Vietnamese counterpart.

My counterpart, *Tu Ta* (which means 'Major') Tran Phi Hai, was most remarkable people I ever met in that war-torn country. Unlike many Vietnamese, *Tu Ta* Hai was incorruptible, at least in my dealing with him, was a devoted family man, had a great sense of humor, and didn't follow the tradition way of thinking of letting the province chief make all the decisions, which could be described as the more traditional Mandarin mindset. He would come up with a good idea, turn it over to my guys that worked for me, and then inform the Province Chief. Since I was never invited – or had any business being there – to these meetings between *Tu Ta* and the big cheese, I don't know what happened, but apparently nothing bad came to *Tu Ta*. In retrospect, I wonder if there were more unique folks like *Tu Ta* Hai, or was he a "one of a kind" man? I also suspect that the did not do well in the "re-education camps" that the North Vietnamese instituted in the South, after they re-invaded the Republic of South Vietnam, contrary to their pledge and signature at the Paris Peace talks. Their actions bring to mind a book I read way back in my earlier academic career titled, "You Can Always Trust a Communist…. To Be a Communist." And now, through *Project Verona*, a de-classified intelligence report from the Kremlin, we are learning more and more how the Soviet Politburo controlled the 'peace and justice' groups in the USA, and how they were the driving force behind all the peace marches and demonstrations. But the worst revelation is that the perfidious testimony of one John Kerry was simply a reading off the play book, directed by the KGB in Moscow. And now this lying POS is our Secretary of State? The world has truly turned upside down.

One of the industries in *Binh Duong* Province was a ceramics factory that made porcelain figures for both domestic and export consumption. Later on, many green porcelain elephant figures would become prominent as end tables or other décor in American homes after the war. Apparently, there was ample availability of clay material in the Province as the factory was steadily producing a great variety of porcelain work. What they really lacked was enough reliable workers; this fact of life and death was another sad legacy that various wars in the region had consumed so much manpower of Vietnam. *Tu Ta* came to me with another great idea: would I be willing to pay a visit to the factory and see if the owner would be willing to hire some of the amputees that lived in town. As a result of land mines, booby traps, small arms fire and a multiple of other devices, there were many amputees from the Army of the Republic of Vietnam soldiers, - ARVN, for short – that lived in *Phu Cuong* City, most of them unemployed or grossly under-employed. With a meager governmental 'safety net' in place, and the resources of the Roman Catholic Church and the *Cao Dai* Temple very limited, most of these amputees had to exist on the extraordinarily small government stipend for their existence. My guess is that they would be happy to have some form of employment, all within the limitations of their respective disabilities.

In the age before the social media, emails, websites, and not much public radio, how the word reached the two dozen ARVN veterans that had gathered outside my office is still a mystery to me. But there they were, and now it was time to fish or cut bait. My Civil Affairs Team had a ¾ ton US Army truck, the most reliable and durable vehicle the Army probably made outside of the WWII Jeep, and it would hold half of the men. *Tu Ta* would have to bring the remainder. And off we convoyed to the porcelain factory, a most unlikely group. Loading and unloading my truck was actually an example of brotherly love, as all the veterans helped one another, no easy task since all of them had at least one limb missing, either an arm or a leg, sometimes multiple missing limbs. While I don't remember the owner's name, I do recall with profound vividness just how he reacted to the truckloads of would-be new employees. He was absolutely ecstatic about the possibility of having more workers, which meant more output which equated to higher profits for him. The ARVN veterans were just as happy, knowing that they would be making a little more money than before. "You take, you take!" the owner of the factory insisted, pointing to a just-made Chinese-style temple dog as a token of his gratitude, I was happy too, to be able to bring home an example of Vietnamese craftsmanship. I was also happy to have been a small cog in the machinery of events that helped some very needy folks.

Towards the end of my assignment to the Advisory Team, I received new orders, transferring me along with my family to Bangkok, Thailand at the end of my tour in Vietnam. Shipping the temple dog to my next home would require some serious packaging, but it got done, thanks to the professionals at the porcelain factory. My family was waiting for me in Taipei, Taiwan, and I was soon on a flight there to get them ready for the subsequent flight to Bangkok, to begin life together again as a united family. Completing all the packing for our trip to Thailand, we entrusted our meager possessions to a freight forwarder for shipment. Included in our shipment were a large number of books that I discovered I could now afford, since Taiwan at the time didn't subscribe to International Copyright standards. A book that would cost $10 back in the States could be had for about $1.25 in Taipei, making the large addition to my personal library well within reach of my captain's pay.

The US Army had contracted with several hotels in Bangkok for both soldiers on R&R, and to house Army folks and their dependents until their household goods had arrived from the States or at least their last duty assignment. My wife and I had stayed in the same hotel during my R&R in December, 1967, so it was a familiar sight when we arrived in January 1971. My "hold baggage" from Vietnam arrived, and I was delighted to see that the temple dog had made the trip completely unscathed! Life seemed to be approaching normalcy with my family and I together again as we waited for our furniture to arrive from Texas. That was until I heard some strange noises in the hallway of the hotel, about 3 weeks into our stay.

Those noises as it turned out, were other hotel guests running down the hall, heading for the stairwell. And the noise was accompanied with the sound of breaking glass, various screams, and other sounds that were unnatural for 3:30 in the morning. Calling downstairs to the front desk produced no results, as I later learned that the front desk personnel and all other hotel employees had long since fled the fire which was now consuming much of the hotel. This was my first introduction to how the Thai customs dramatically conflicted with ours. As I opened my hotel room door to look down the hallway, I saw a wall of fire that was rapidly moving my way along the teak paneling that covered the walls. Closing the door quickly, I rushed to awaken our two children and proceeded to get them ready for the only other means of escape – jumping out of the window to the ground below.

As it turned out, all of us made it out of the hotel safely, including the family dog. We escaped with the clothing we had on and little else. I did manage to throw one suitcase out the window that still had some unpacked clothing for my wife and children. But there were over 20 fatalities, including an American family of a mustached husband, a blond wife, and 2 children, a boy and a girl. This description fit my family perfectly, and when I finally found the place where all Americans were to report, my sponsor almost fainted as he had heard that we had all perished in the fire! I assured him that we were quite alive and well, albeit with multiple bruises and sprains from our escape from the fire.

Two days later, the survivors were allowed back into the hotel to see if there was anything salvageable from the ruins. All of our clothing was burned, all of the books were either burned or water-logged beyond redemption, but my temple dog was still recognizable even though it had a layer of black soot on it about ¼ inch thick. That soot reminded me that had we stayed in the room, our corpses would have had that same soot, inside the lungs and coating our bodies. To this day, I Thank my Lord for guiding us out of that furnace of death. Carrying my temple dog out of the hotel ruins, I headed to my new residence, a house I had rented the day before, and handed my treasure to one of the maids. Since I didn't speak much Thai that early in my tour, I simply found a scrub brush, a can of Ajax, and told her to clean it. She got the message.

AFTERWORD: Now, after moving to 15 or so different houses or apartments in and around Texas, this temple dog is still on point, guarding my home near Dripping Springs, Texas. It serves as a reminder of how that little factory in *Phu Cuong* City served as a microcosm of humanity and how a few completely different folks came to work together for a common goal. There were no losers in this situation – a beautiful scenario of "win-win." I'm deeply grateful for that example and for the temple dog as well. This event reminded me of the beginning of a famous book, "… it was the best of times, and it was the worst of times….." Doubtless, we could apply that lesson in cooperatively living in America. I truly despise the polarization that has occurred and is occurring in America, its intensity growing with every day it seems. I have to ask myself, are we losing the opportunity to have reasoned, sensible dialogue? Or has it already gone away?

Teaching Ethics on the Fly

SOME TEN YEARS after my second tour in Vietnam, I was serving as the S-3 or Operations and Training Officer for an armor battalion which was part of the Texas Army National Guard. During one week-end drill, I was talking to our battalion chaplain, who mentioned that he was teaching a class in Ethics at Concordia Lutheran College in Austin, Texas, I jokingly asked, "Why don't you invite me to give a talk on 'Ethics of the Battlefield' to your class?" To my surprise, he said that would be a great idea, and could I show up next Tuesday at 1400 hours, and be in Class A uniform, please! I had just learned, or re-learned for the umpteenth time that being a smart-ass could get me in trouble, but now I had to 'put up or shut up!'

Preparing for this class, I remembered four distinct and separate incidences where 'ethics' were involved, one with a pineapple, one with an interfering general, one involving a pagoda, and one with several NVA potential prisoners of war – hardly subject matter for any lessons in ethics, or so it would seem! But stay tuned.

On a very routine patrol one beautiful day, my platoon encountered a very remote farm a bit off the beaten path. Besides the ubiquitous rice paddies, the farmer had a few row crops of beans and other vegetables, and several pine-apple plants. As I wrote in another vignette, the pineapples of Vietnam were absolutely the best I had ever eaten, and for me, still form the culinary paragon upon which other pine-apples are judged and compared. So after carefully searching the farmer's modest abode, and receiving assurances that he wasn't a VC, we departed his farm for other places to search. About 50 yards out from the farm, I glanced back at the line of my soldiers, checking to see if they were still spread out per SOP, still alternating weapons' directions per SOP, and generally complying with the patrol order. Everyone was do-ing what was expected of them, except one soldier who was busy peeling a pineapple while carrying his weapon at sling arms, not the usual patrol posture. Halting the patrol, I walked back to my roving gourmet, and inquired about the origins of his exquisitely smelling pineapple. "Back at that farm," was his reply, in all quasi-innocence. I immediately ordered the patrol to head back to the farm. As we neared the farmer's modest hootch, he exited from his chores, appearing quite frightened. I motioned for my felonious gourmand to come forward. "How much did you pay him for this pineapple?" I asked him. "I just took it," was his reply. Another question from me: "How much money do you have on you?" His walled, wrapped in a discarded plastic battery wrapper re-vealed about $5 in MPC, Military Payment Certificates, which we were issued in lieu of 'greenbacks.' "Give it to the farmer," was my next order. After much discussion between the farmer and me, I was able to convince him that (1) my men didn't steal from the Vietnamese, and (2) that my soldier was sorry that he forgot my guidelines. After paying the farmer for the most expensive pineapple in recorded Vietnamese history, I ordered the patrol to resume the mission. Walking next to my now penniless soldier, I told him that that pineapple that he stole might have been the only food the farmer's family had for that day. I also reminded him of the more practical reality that by pissing off the farmer by our bad manners, he might just want to give aid and comfort to the enemy in a manner of his own choosing, which didn't bode well for us. "We have enough enemy around us, and we don't need to be making any more of them by acting stupid and stealing their food. Got it?" Ethics Lesson #1 on the fly: Don't steal and don't give the locals a chance to hate you.

Especially for the enlisted men, sometimes officers can be a royal pain in the ass. And for junior officers, sometimes generals can be that same irritant! On one particular day, while we were minding our own business on a routine patrol, I got a radio call, "Panther Romeo 6, this is Antelope 6!" Who the hell is 'Antelope 6', I asked myself? Back in the 60's, all commanders, from platoon leader to company commander to battalion commander, all the way up the food chain, had the numerical suffix of "6". So I knew it was some commander that I didn't recognize. Quickly scanning my CEOI – "Communications-Electronics Operating Instructions" – I learned that it was the Assistant Division Commander, Brigadier General Yarbrough! "Antelope 6, this is Panther Romeo 6" I replied. His next instructions only reinforced an earlier perception I had of him: not too bright, but looked good in starched fatigues. "There are some fresh diggings up on that hill to your immediate northeast. It might be a bunker complex, and we can't have the enemy that close to our logistics base! Take your unit up there and check it out!" The area in question had been – and I stress the past tense – had been a VC bunker complex dating back to the days of the Viet Minh, some 20+ years ago, and was located just a quarter of a mile away from *Long Binh*. It had been searched, sanitized, re-searched, and scoured countless times, resulting in no VC in the area for at least a generation. The 'fresh diggings' reported by General Bright Star were actually the results of excess ordnance from US aircraft being dropped there before they returned to *Bien Hoa* Air Base. It seems that pilots, and even more so, their ground crews, don't like to land with bombs hanging off the wings, so a designated disposal area was the old VC bunker complex. "This is Antelope 6: you people look too bunched up down there! You need to get into a tactical formation and get up that hill!" By this time, I was getting a bit steamed, and not just from the weather. I had a small writing pad stuck into one of my fatigue pants' pockets and pulled out the pad, ripped out a page of paper, and started crumpling it up, right at the mouthpiece of my radio handset. "Antelope 6, this is Panther Romeo 6, your last is broken and garbled!" But in between every word, a sound of crumpling paper marvelously imitated a really bad radio connection. The next sound I heard was the most welcome one of the day: "This is Antelope 6 Out!" With that, Brigadier General Yarbrough flew back to his air-conditioned office at Camp Bearcat, while I halted my little patrol, gave them the order to stand-down, and return to the our tracks. Once we got back to where the tracks and drivers were waiting for us, I gathered the Scouts around and gave them an explanation of what just happened. "Guys, we all know what's up on that hill, and some big muckeeteemuck wanted us to go up there and search for Charlie. There hasn't been a Cong up there since 1954, and I didn't want to participate in a useless exercise, when we could be pulling some much need vehicle maintenance on our tracks! I just used a radio trick I learned several months ago about how to make it sound like the radio isn't working well, and I guess the general got tired of trying to communicate with me so he left. All you need to know is that we had radio troubles, in case anybody ever asks. Now get to work pulling the maintenance on the tracks, including the track tension!" <u>Ethics Lesson #2</u> on the fly: Remember what's important!

Even the war in Vietnam was not immune from having its share of "Springbucks." Normally confined to the States, and in garrison or camp environments and in military schools, a "springbuck" is usually a company-grade officer who has the answer to any given question, and if a question hasn't been asked, he'll make up a situation, and then provide the solution. In a classroom environment, he's the first person with his hand in the air offering an answer, primarily to hear the sound of his own mellifluous voice. "Springbucks" invariably are the sole source of really stupid ideas that some moron a little further up the food chain tries to put into action, so they become a self-fulfilling situation of lunacy. In 1967, we even had a full colonel who could have won the prize for Springbuck of the Year award.

Our battalion was operating in an area that had been sanitized quite thoroughly by elements of the 1st Infantry Division before they were moved to another Area of Operation. But we were still required to do the normal amount of patrolling, to set up night ambushes, and all the other latent defensive tactics normal to an infantry unit. OK so far! Then the Good Idea Fairy struck the Brigade Commander who decided that we needed to conduct <u>night combat patrols</u>! You heard me right, <u>night combat patrols</u>! "Here's the plan, men, we thrash around in the jungle at night, where we can't see our hands in front of our faces, and we sneak up on Charlie, who hasn't been here in years, knows the area if he's here at all, and if we don't fall into a punji pit first! And then he shoots us, when we can't even see him, and vanishes into the night! Doesn't that sound like fun? Gee whiz, just like they do in all the war movies!" That was the scenario we found ourselves in with the Colonel Bright Idea's edict that every rifle company send out at least one night combat patrol each evening.

And soon enough, it was the 3rd Platoon's time to participate in this Exercise of Greatest Futility! After I had received the company patrol order, which included a set of Check Points, a pre-arranged set of radio handset signals, and other coordinating instructions, I called my squad leaders together to give them the patrol order. "In addition to the normal combat load, I want every man to carry a Claymore or a trip flare" I instructed the squad leaders. "Lieutenant, how can we use a Claymore or a trip flare on a night combat patrol?" came the question from my stunned sub-ordinate leaders. "Just trust me for now, and I'll explain later," was my reply, along with the order to be ready to move out at 1830 hours.

Our first Check Point was an old deserted pagoda, right on the map where it was supposed to be. We arrived there with just enough light to allow the men to set up the Claymores and trip flares. I halted the patrol, and had all the men assemble around me. "Here's the plan: instead of thrashing around in the woods tonight, we're going to spend the night here. Normally, I obey all orders given, but this one we're just going to modify slightly so nobody gets hurt because of somebody else's stupidity." The squad leaders were given instructions to form a tight security ring around the pagoda, to have the men set out the Claymore mines and trip flares, and to pull a "50-50" for the night. In each fighting position, 50% of the men were awake and on guard, while the other 50% slept, and then these positions were swapped about midnight. Between my radio-telephone operator (RTO), the platoon medic and the 4.2" mortar forward observer and me, we would form our own little team and call in the requisite Check Points.

Near daybreak, I called for 100% stand-to, and instructed the squad leaders to get ready to retrieve the Claymores and trip flares. When there was enough daylight, this task was done, and then it was time to 'ruck up' and head back to the company position, by a different route of course. Maybe some would question my decision to disregard the requirement of having conducted a moving, night-time combat patrol, but the safety of my men transcended any useless order that I might have received. Even if this operation had been an area crawling with VC, I probably would have made the same decision, because at the time, the night belonged to Charlie, as we didn't have the night-time, whiz-bang technology that exists today. All we would have done was incur senseless casualties, while trying to make some bird colonel look good. That level of stupidity didn't work with me then, and shouldn't work for some colonel now. If I did something wrong, then I stand convicted. But the lives and welfare of my men, who I had the honor of commanding and leading, was too important to jeopardize because of some fool who had never been in the jungle, much less knew how Charlie operated. I thank my God for giving me the discernment to make what I still consider to be the right decision. Ethics Lesson #3 on the fly: Practice God-given discernment, and take care of your men, as they are your most precious weapon!

During the Tet Counter-Offensive, the Scout Platoon captured over 30 North Vietnamese soldiers in the battle of Widows' Village. Although this was a very unusual event, the Scouts had been well instructed long before my tenure as their leader on the proper handling of prisoners of war. This period of instruction speaks to the very core of Army values, and my Scouts had learned it well. While we were in the midst of the battle, a lone lieutenant colonel from II Field Forces – a major US Army headquarters that was right across the highway from the current battle - showed up and sought me out as the ranking man on the ground. He came equipped with an M-14, one magazine of ammunition, a flak jacket that looked like it was straight out of the shipping box, and the cleanest camouflage cover on his helmet that I had ever seen. A real warrior, um hmm. We had not yet completely 'sanitized' the battlefield, meaning that there were still some wounded NVA soldiers who had not yet been disarmed so that we could take them prisoner. My attitude, as was that of the Scouts, is that if an enemy combatant has any means of harming one of my men, be it in the form of an AK-47, hand grenade, knife, stick or rock, he was still an enemy combatant and would be treated as such. But the second that he had no more means of resistance or was no longer any threat, he became a prisoner of war, and how he was treated also changed instantaneously. This rule was applied later in the day, when we discovered more than 30 North Vietnamese soldiers in a culvert, and took almost every one of them prisoner. Every Scout knew my rules, and also knew that there was no equivocation in the enforcement of those rules. Some things in life are indeed distinctly black and white, and this was one of them.

"Grenade!" The screamed warning was heeded by everybody, including our transient lieutenant colonel. One NVA soldier had a "potato masher" type of grenade and had tossed it a few feet away after pulling the string and activating the grenade. Immediately after the explosion, SSG Allen Mutchler jumped to his feet, ready to eliminate any enemy threat he could see. Armed with an M-60 machine gun and at least a 100-round belt of ammunition, Mutchler was ready for just about anything. When the same NVA tried to repeat his hand grenade defense, Mutchler convinced him to do otherwise with an eight-round burst. The lieutenant colonel, who had not seen the attempt to arm the second grenade, began to admonish me for shooting unarmed prisoners. Just about that time, a second explosion nearby caught us all off guard, and in the process, the lieutenant colonel caught a piece of gravel or some form of projectile in the fleshy part of his right cheek. The trickle of blood and trickle may be an overstatement, coursed down his cheek about ½ inch, and promptly stopped. He wasn't even aware of it, so I said, "It looks like you caught some shrapnel!" With that, the lieutenant colonel wiped his cheek with his hand, saw the blood, and with eyes very wide open, fled back to his comfy and safe little office at II Field Forces, probably to write himself up for a Purple Heart and a Silver Star. Ethics Lesson #4 on the fly: Remember the Laws of Land Warfare, and make sure your men know them as well or better than you do!

The gratitude for these lessons extends to all my Scouts, to Chaplain Ron Jones, and to my Awesome Creator, Who blessed me then with discernment, courage, understanding and a healthy dose of common sense.

Tet 1968
Reflective Thoughts - 2008

FORTY YEARS AGO – a lifetime for some – a lifetime never realized by others – and an eternity for still others – an event occurred, so primal, so coarse, and so epochal that it has become the benchmark of our lives. From that cauldron of chaos, that crucible of inhuman intensity arose a rare form of union that makes us different. We are no better than others who were there - the company clerk, the finance officer, or the countless other support personnel – not better, just different. We have withstood the very worst that inhumanity can force upon human beings, and we have maintained our sanity, our sense of purpose, and sometime even our sense of humor.

We have moved forward to our own individual series of victories, sometimes interspersed with failures, creating lives for ourselves, striving to become what Our Creator intended us to be. We have walked the hollow streets of commerce, the hallowed halls of Congress, and the holy fields of grain and cattle, not better than our neighbors, only different. And there is that small part within all of us that draws us like a moth to a flame - to that Day of Days that makes us different.

We remember who we were, and who we have become. We remember those whose shortened lives made us more sensitive to the living. While we mourn their death, we give thanks for their service, and for that rare opportunity to have been in their presence, if only briefly. We remember all that we have accomplished, and are reminded of exciting challenges that lie ahead. We give thanks for all our blessings while striving to make the world a better place.

It is indeed an honorable thing to defend one's country from threatening forces. Perhaps it is not only honorable, but one's sacred duty. This, among other reasons, is why I hold our WWII veterans and our current crop of warriors in such high esteem. And it is even more noble, more sacrificial, and enormously more difficult, to fight for another country's freedoms and liberties. Such were our sacrifices in Vietnam, a land threatened and later overwhelmed by communist tyranny. In its stifling of individual freedoms, its denial of basic human rights, and its deadly response to any opposition, the communists have always erected barriers to any exodus. The Berlin Wall, the Iron Curtain and the Bamboo Curtain were not built to keep people out of the Workers' Paradise. Over the decades of communism's repressive reign, millions of people have tried, fewer millions have succeeded, and tragically, other millions have died trying to flee and find freedom and liberty, much like we enjoy today. Despite the eventual deceit of the North Vietnamese Army and their re-invasion of Vietnam, we few, we happy few, we band of brothers, bled, suffered and watched our brothers die in our valiant efforts to bring and maintain liberty in a foreign land. Our sacrifice, our noble cause, was totally misinterpreted, treated with scorn and contempt, while we began to doubt ourselves. But the passage of time and the silencing of shrill animus have been followed by the thoughtful and reflective realization, and now acknowledgement and appreciation of who we were, and what we accomplished. We were the warriors, standing in the breach of the wall of decency and human dignity, repelling the barbarians at the gate. We few, we noble few, can stand tall and justified by the reality of our sacrifices, by the dignity of our efforts, and by the integrity of our goals. We bow to no man, but humbly offer ourselves, our fortunes, and our sacred honor to our Almighty God in gratitude for the privilege of serving this great nation.

As Best I Remembered It: My Recollections of the Battle for Widows' Village, Tet 1968

[An highly-edited version of this account appeared in the February 2014 issue of the *Vietnam* Magazine]

IN ORDER TO comply with the directive to maintain a low profile during the upcoming Tet celebration, our mechanized infantry battalion had been ordered to set up in a position off Highway 15, the major road leading to the port city of *Vung Tau*. All offensive operations were also put on hold during this ceasefire period. And although few of us understood the significance of the Tet celebration in the Vietnamese culture, we were looking forward to some slack time. But such was not to be!

Shortly before sunset, a change of mission for the battalion immediately set in motion a series of actions that caused us to dismantle our defensive position, to load all concertina wire, engineer stakes, and other material, and head towards *Long Binh*, a huge logistical base northeast of Saigon. My platoon, the battalion Scouts, consisting of ten armored personnel carriers, upgraded to ACAV's, with gun shields around the .50 caliber MG, gun shields for side-mounted M60 MG's, and two ACAV's equipped with 106mm recoilless rifles. The Scouts were directed to a position south of *Long Binh* along the Highway 15, ready to respond to any calls from the battalion commander. The longest day of my life was about to begin.

The night progressed smoothly and without incident, with all of my tracks calling a negative situation report or SITREP until 0400 hours, when I monitored an excited voice from the Military Police in Saigon, who coincidentally shared our radio frequency. I heard that the VC had stolen two MP jeeps. The next obvious question that came to my mind was, "Just what the hell were VC doing in Saigon during this celebration?" From that time on, our net became a constant clutter of calls, all reporting various stages of street fighting in Saigon. Not long after this, I heard that the VC [only later did I learn that the enemy was regular North Vietnamese forces, not Viet Cong] were occupying positions inside the US Embassy, and that our troops were being lifted on to the roof to combat these forces.

Very shortly after the first light of dawn began to creep over the bamboo lining our particular sector of the highway, my platoon was ordered to move to the vicinity of the 90th Replacement Battalion, picking up the battalion command element enroute. As we arrived there, I monitored the transmission between Companies A and C, and the battalion commander, or the Old Man. Turning around to verify the arrival of the trail track, I saw a huge ball of fire, preceded by a racing shock wave, erupting from the 3rd Ordnance Battalion Ammunition Supply Depot, about a mile to the east. Several more satchel charges, with attached timing devices, were later discovered within the depot area, and had it not been for the ineptitude of the NVA sappers, these charges could have done enormous damage.

As we continued to monitor the progress of the battles that involved all of the line companies, we were getting more and more excited, anxious and ready to assist our buddies. Not long afterwards, a medic drove his ambulance to our location, and begged us to give him some assistance with some casualties and others who were pinned down by the enemy. I tried to explain to him that I just couldn't follow him, as my orders came from my battalion commander. Just then, the voice of Panther 6, the Old Man, came over my radio, ordering me to move to the vicinity of II Field Forces Headquarters. The medic followed us to our new location, and continued to plead for assistance. I decided to ask the Old Man for permission to perform this rescue and relief mission, as the casualties and unit in question were close. He told me to detach two of my ACAV's to help secure the battalion tactical operations center, and then to proceed with the requested mission. With an affirmative answer from Panther 6 still ringing in my ear, we raced for Widows' Village. The longest day of my life was about to become extraordinarily more complicated.

As the medic pointed us in the direction of the beleaguered American unit, I counted four APC's on the edge of this small hamlet, with one sitting on the road blocking our entrance. At this time, I couldn't detect much incoming fire, and no outgoing friendly fire, but did notice several troops crouching beside the APC on our route. I dismounted my APC, and noticed that no one was in the track commander's (TC's) hatch, manning the .50 caliber MG, SOP during combat operations. Then I saw that the TC had been killed, and others in his squad were wounded, and trying to form a fighting position beside the disabled track. Calling for my medic to start treating the wounded, I hand-signaled my other tracks to start deploying into a line formation on either side of the disabled track, and to start counter-attacking the enemy forces before us.

Normally, when confronted with what appears to be superior firepower, fortified positions and a poor force ratio, I would call for indirect fire support, air strikes, or some form of combat equalizer or combat multiplier. The voice at Panther 33, our Net Control Station, informed me that all indirect fires were denied in this area due to the proximity of civilians. This denial of assistance was not a good sign, but we pressed on. The lack of indirect fire support was going to make this a very long and dangerous day. We began to move forward by fire and movement, with either side of the attacking line alternating their fire and running forward. Soon we reached a ditch line where snipers had been hiding and began a systematic elimination of their fighting effectiveness. It was at this early stage in what became the longest day of my military career that I encountered what was to become a series of miracles. I was walking back to my track to get more ammunition when I noticed movement in the ditch to my immediate left, at a distance of less than ten feet. I was under the mistaken impression that we had cleared and swept past this point, eliminating all enemy presence, and had paused to re-establish the skirmish line. In what seemed like a slow-motion process, an NVA soldier raised his AK-47, pointing it right at me. Without having to aim, I fired off a round, seeing it hit him in the chest; the only reaction from him was reflexive, as he fell back against the back of the ditch, and started aiming his weapon at me again. After two more well placed shots, he finally went to his reward, while at the same instant, another soldier, just to his left, started the exact same procedure. As I pulled the trigger to take him out, all I heard was the "click" indicating that the bolt was locked to the rear position, and I was out of ammo.

Knowing that I didn't possibly have time to reload, I spun around in the classic pivot-kick that I had learned in Basic Combat Training, knocking the weapon out of his hands, and took him prisoner. Why I was spared, when I should have become a casualty, became the initial "Angel Tap" for me to start paying attention to greater and more important things that lay head in my life.

What we were up against soon became apparent: weapons ranged from AK-47's, heavy machine guns (.51 caliber), RPD light MG's, and rocket propelled grenades (RPG's). From the volume of fire we were receiving, I realized that this was not simply a small-unit ambush, the typical contact we usually encountered. This was a large force, at least company-sized, well organized, well entrenched, and about to overrun and annihilate the American unit we rescued, a mechanized rifle platoon that was reduced to less than 15 combat-effective fighters. Their platoon leader [a 1LT Henry Jezek, another Texan, who would later lead the Scouts after my departure] was already gravely wounded, and the remaining warriors were fighting valiantly against overwhelming odds. Apparently, we showed up at the right moment!

After overrunning what were the enemy's outposts, we continued the attack through the village, only to encounter rolls of concertina wire that were strung along the limits of the yards. Our textbook mounted and dismounted attack was about to come to a grinding halt, until some Scouts, SSG George Ottesen, SSG Junious Hayes, SSG Robert Mutchler, SP4 Ray Rehfeldt and SP4 Bill McCaskill, without direction or orders from me, low-crawled through incoming fire, wire cutters in hand, and created openings for our ACAV's. While this wire clearing operations was taking place, the grenadiers continued to place a high volume of fire on suspected or confirmed enemy locations. Our .50 caliber MG's and M-60's continued to provide suppressing fires to protect our wire cutters. As the fire became more intense and effective, a Vietnamese woman with two small children suddenly appeared, directly to our front, on the dirt road that ran between two rows of houses. Obviously, she was in a state of panic, uncertain of where to go to avoid being killed. Friendly fires instantaneously were re-directed away from her area. I shouted for her to come forward to safety, assuming she could understand me or even hear me, but fear held her back. In order to remove them from the danger area, I ran forward and carried all three of them to safety behind one of our ACAV's. As I was carrying her and her two children back to a safe place, I heard the crack of small arms all around me, and saw the dirt kicked up to either side of us as bullets came near. I was aware at that time of the presence of a "blue veil" that had enveloped me, although I was not certain when this Divine Protection first was made known to me. Only much later did I realize that I had been the direct recipient of a genuine miracle. As long as that "blue veil" was surrounding me, as it appeared to do from head to foot, no harm could come to me or to those around me in the immediate proximity. Nor could I do any wrong, or say any wrong. I don't recall even having the ability to curse at the time, which certainly would have seemed to be the soldier's prerogative, considering the circumstances in which I found myself. The gift of Grace, in a very active sense, became the wellspring of my realization of other miracles that have subsequently occurred in my life, and the absolute certainty that other miracles will occur in the future. When the woman and her two children were secure, we renewed the attack, crushing several hootches along the way, thereby denying their use to the enemy. All resistance on this sweep was eliminated, and another sweep was begun. On the second sweep, several more prisoners were taken, and more weapons and equipment was seized. I returned to my track, wanting desperately to have some time to regroup my thoughts, to plan for the next phase, and maybe to have a quick smoke. Instead of the calm I was seeking, I found confusion, fear, and my driver, SP4 Danny Lawless, holding the near-lifeless body of SP4 Charles Kronberg. During my absence while leading the just completed assault, Kronberg had climbed into the cupola of my ACAV, and began to fire the .50 caliber MG to cover our movement in the attack. Chuck had been shot in the head, and my medic, SP4 Paul Keener and Lawless were fighting desperately to save his life. I saw the gaping wound in the back of his head and the patches of black blood, and walked away in sickness that such a fine your man died in the nondescript place of "Widows' Village." His eyes were already glazed over in the "death stare," and I had to turn away. My sense of helplessness was the realization that there was nothing I could for Chuck. And I recall the look of total helplessness in the eyes of Lawless, who had been a close friend of Chuck's, eyes that pleaded for me to do something. But this was not the time for tears, melancholy or despair, as a variety of snipers was still bringing us under fire.

At one point during the day, we were attempting to sort out the enemy wounded form the prisoners, and to prepare for the next phase of the operation. During this lull in the action, I directed my medics to start treating the wounded POW's. I had heard that the NVA had propagandized their troops into believing that, if captured, the Americans would torture and maim them beyond belief. As "Doc" Keener opened his aid bag, exposing the neatly arranged surgical instruments, I could see the look of pure panic in the eyes of the POW's. For good reason. Inside the Aid Bag was an assortment of forceps, scalpels, and other surgical devices the use of which I care not to know! But then Keener gently cut the torn and bloody sleeve away of the first one, so that he could dress the wound, the look of terror was slowly replaced by one of relief and gratitude. Shortly after this triage session, a group of MP's, to include a captain, a sergeant and two specialists, arrived on what appeared to be a tourist ride; they sat in their jeep, taking pictures, and acting like a bunch of tourists on vacation. One of the wounded enemy soldiers was pulled out of a nearby pipe culvert, and still not convinced that he would be better off as a prisoner, pulled the string on the "potato masher" Chi-Com grenade, thereby activating the trigger mechanism, and tossed it in the general vicinity of some of my Scouts. When one of my men saw this, he yelled, "Grenade!" and everybody hit the ground, the safest place to be in an instant like this. After the smoke and dust cleared from this grenade, which did no harm to any of my Scouts, one of the MP's took his weapon, flipped the switch to full automatic, and fired off a full magazine in the general direction of the now disarmed NVA soldier, missing him completely, but hitting PFC Richard Veilbaum, a newly arrived Scout, in the neck, killing him almost instantly. I arrived on the scene about two minutes after this act of complete stupidity had occurred, and been over in another part of the village coordinating the actions of the supporting attack. One of my Scouts, Bill McCaskill, told me what had happened, and seeing the absolute white rage that was surrounding him and my other troops, I told the MP captain that his safety in my area could only be guaranteed for the next fifteen seconds, as at least five .50 caliber MG's, and other weaponry were pointed in his direction. To his everlasting credit, the captain and his sorry bunch of MP's quickly departed, thereby avoiding what might have been yet another senseless tragedy. [Years later, I learned that the same captain had confessed to Keith W. Nolan, author of *The Battle for Saigon*, which contains this story, that he had been the guilty party at that shooting, and that he had carried this guilt for 40+ years. I have since forgiven him too.]

Later that morning, I noticed two gunships continually circling our position. We were still in heavy contact with the NVA, and I knew that this firepower, if available, would help us break the fierce resistance we were encountering. These were Cobras, and I had never seen them employed in a fire mission before, as they had only recently arrived in country. Since I didn't have either their call sign or radio frequency, I resorted to simple hand-and-arm signals to direct them to where they were needed. Despite the incoming fire, I decided to stand on top of ACAV, and pulled on my collar, pointing that I was the ranking man on the ground. I saw the command pilot of the lead ship nod his head in agreement, as he made another orbit around our position. On his second pass, I pointed down a row of houses that I wanted him to fire upon, then drew my finger across my throat, to signify slicing, and he nodded agreement again. On the third pass, the firing began, with the automatic grenade launcher and miniguns making a powerful statement of newly arrive military technology, which I appreciated by getting off the top of my APC. Following several gun runs, we swept through that portion of the village, counting more enemy dead, gathering more weapons and equipment. Two hours later, as we were replenishing our ammo supplies, I noticed a stranger walking up to my ACAV, a short pudgy man wearing a flight suit, a .38 caliber slung like Wyatt Earp, and a brand new camouflage cover on his steel pot, complete with "bird" colonel insignia. Naturally, I saluted smartly as a lieutenant does not encounter a full colonel every day! Rather cockily he asked, "How did you like the gunship support this morning?" I automatically assumed that he was the lead pilot, and hastily replied, "Right on target, sir!" Then I asked him if he had any trouble understanding my hand-and-arm signals. "Hell no, lieuten-ant, I knew exactly what you meant!" My follow-on question was more important: in the event I need him again, what was his call sign and radio frequency? "Checkmate 44, on FM 62.25." Names and numbers forever burned into my psyche.

By now, everyone had replenished their supply of ammo, so I dismounted my APC one more time to direct the final assault in Widows' Village. I wanted to mass the fires of our .50 caliber MG's, the M-60 MG's, M-79 grenade launchers, and anything else I could deliver in this assault to perma-nently rid Widows' Village of the NVA. We were not able to find any ammo for our recoilless rifles, or to secure any indirect fire support, so our attack would only involve our organic weaponry. I had already coordinated this final push with Company B of the 4th Battalion, 39th Infantry, who had been airlifted into a position on our far left flank, and they were prepared for my signal to begin. All eight of my ACAV's, plus the two APC's from 1st Platoon, Co. B, were positioned in a line formation, with dismounted troops in between them. On my pre-arranged signal, all weapons roared into action, spewing suppressing fire, death and destruction to any NVA still hiding in ditches, bushes, hootches, or rubble. In less than 10 minutes, all resistance was crushed; we consolidated our position, and prepared for the next mission from Panther 6. I noticed the severe ringing in my ear due to the intense noise of eight .50 caliber MG's, 16 M-60 MG's, and numerous other small arms, all firing simultaneously. (This tinnitus has continued to this day.) Walking back to my track through a part of the village, I encountered enemy dead and wounded, who were casualties of either our ground fire or that of the helicopter gunships I had called in earlier. One NVA soldier in particular was a recipient of the gun ship's power, having been blown into two pieces, with the upper part of his torso separated by about fifteen feet from what was left of him. The stench of blood, shit, fear, dirt, gunpowder, and a few dozen other elements was almost enough to make me wretch. By this time, several ambulances and some cooperative MP's had arrived, and relieved us of the burden and responsibility of treating and securing the30+ prisoners of war that we had taken.

After clearing Widows' Village of all NVA my platoon was ordered to assist our Company C, who had been in heavy contact with NVA forces around Bien Hoa Air Base. To get there, we had to go through Ho Nai village, a cluster of tightly packed shops, stores and hootches along Highway 1. This village was predominately Roman Catholic, being made up of refugees from North Vietnam who had fled south to avoid the religious persecution of the communists. I had failed to comprehend the depth of the infiltration of the NVA, or their respective strength in the area. Before all eight of my tracks could clear the village, we were caught in a murderous ambush that cut my platoon into three groups, each confronting its own numerically superior enemy force. We had been suckered into the classic NVA/VC ambush pattern, with RPG's, heavy machine guns, and roadblocks. Our mission to assist Charlie Company was now replaced by a more urgent mission of extricating ourselves from this kill zone. One RPG round landed right behind my track and the resulting concussion slammed me against the right side of the cargo hatch, injuring my right shoulder and right knee. Some of the shrapnel found its way into the right side of my neck, I discovered later. Under the circumstances I found myself, it seems that sweat and blood generally have the same temperature, and under the stress of combat, I didn't realize the extent of my injuries until much later at the Battalion Aid Station.

Per SOP, we stopped in a herringbone pattern to provide as

much interlocking and mutually supporting fires as possible. In the front group, McCaskill and Lawless quickly dismounted an M-60 MG to establish a security element to our exposed left front. They successfully thwarted several attempts by the enemy to flank us and to infiltrate our position. Radio calls from other tracks told me the rest of the story, with casualty reports, current situation, and calls for assistance. In the lead element, our situation stabilized with the heroic actions of McCaskill and Lawless, while Keener was maneuvering to assist the middle element. In a crouching run, carrying his aid bag and his M-16, Keener had almost made it to a semi-secure location to treat casualties in the middle group when he took an AK-47 round in the right temple side of his helmet. Sprawled on the highway in front of the Catholic Church, Keener lay bleeding, and having seen him get hit, I thought he was dead, until I heard his cursing like a man possessed! I low-crawled to his location and dragged him back to my ACAV where we applied two individual wound dressings to his severe head wound. Meanwhile, in the rearmost section of my platoon, MAJ Ray Funderburk, the 9th Infantry Division Public Affairs Officer, was recording more heroic actions in sight and sound. Funderburk, who had linked up with us in Widows' Village, had hitched a ride with us after hearing of our exploits there. Taking charge of the situation, Funderburk directed the fires of the Scouts to the various machine gun nests, RPG sites, and other enemy positions that were threatening to overrun his small force. He later related to me that one of his men, 1LT Charles Ashton, a photographer from Granite City, California, played an integral part in the successful defense of our "rear echelon." Charles was ordered to take an M-60 and a couple of belts of ammo and to set up a flanking fire position on the enemy stronghold. Ashton had expended an entire belt of ammo when he was wounded in his left hand, with the bullet traveling up his arm and exiting out his back. Funderburk was able to administer first aid to stop the bleeding, and to arrange for his evacuation to a field hospital. Ashton spent a couple of months in a US Army hospital in Japan recuperating from his wounds, before returning to duty with the 9th Infantry Division Public Information Office. For his actions, Ashton was awarded a Purple Heart, and will be made an Honorary Scout at the next 47th Infantry Regimental Reunion. Maj Ray Funderburk was later awarded the Silver Star for his heroic actions in rallying the Scouts and members of his PIO Team into an effective fighting force that prevented the Scout section from being overrun by a numerically superior enemy force.

SSG Robert Schultz had dismounted his APC to charge a MG team that was placing deadly fire on a disabled track; after successfully eliminating this threat, Schultz charged another MG nest, throwing hand grenades and firing a captured AK-47, falling mortally wounded after destroying this second threat. Meanwhile, SP4 Lee Wilson spotted an RPG site that was firing on another APC, and calmly standing in the middle of Highway 1, with bullets and RPG's landing all around him, fired a Light, Anti-Armor, Weapon (LAW) into the exact location of the RPG team, sending them to their reward.

Fighting house-to-house, we were able to successfully link up with the middle element, retrieved and treated the wounded, and tried for a Dust-Off mission. When the Medevac copter was on final approach, I ordered him out of our area, as he was taking intense ground fire from other enemy positions, and I didn't need four more casualties to add to what I already had. We continued our extraction process, linking up with the trail element in preparation to executing an assault on the remaining RPG nest. A call to Checkmate 44 brought two gunships, old, reliable Huey B models, to provide us some suppressive fires. Directing them to the target, this time with radio contact, we witnessed the devastating effect of a full load of 2.75" rockets from both gunships, utterly destroying the yellow two-story house. Complying with the directives of Panther 6, we raced to his location to rejoin other elements of the Battalion, and to secure treatment for our wounded.

After reaching the battalion location and getting the wounded to the Aid Station, I started checking on the remainder of my warriors. It was only at this time that I was told that SSG Schultz had been killed, and was still in the village of *Ho Nai*. I could only begin to feel the loss of this fine young hero, as he had been a recent and very welcome addition to my platoon, and the old-timers respected and admired his professionalism, sense of humor, and complete devotion to his subordinates. I reported to the TOC, and told them that I was going back to Ho Nai to retrieve his body. At this point, I was crying, partly from a sense of rage of having any of my men killed, partly for a plea for relief, and partly because I just didn't know how else to deal with the insanity that I had just witnessed. Panther 6, not known to be the most affectionate person in the world, knew exactly what to do, grabbed and hugged me, letting me sob unashamedly. He told me that it would serve no useful purpose to expose my men to further harm at that time, and that he understood the need to go back there, but that I would return to *Ho Nai* the next morning, and that was an order.

The following morning, we slowly walked down the middle of Highway 1, the road we had driven down the day before, right into the longest ambush I had ever encountered. We met several civilians who had returned to their village, still warning us of *"beaucoup VC,"* but we did not meet any resistance. There were several dead NVA lying beside the road, indications that the surviving enemy forces left in a hurry, as they normally extracted their dead with them. About one-half mile into the village from our start point, we found the body of SSG Schultz, which had been carried out from the interior of the village where he had fallen, by some Vietnamese Catholic nuns, whose church was right across the street. The most beautiful lace handkerchief had been placed over his face, and I called for my track to come forward, so he could have his final ride as a real Scout.

Afterward: An examination of documents related to Enemy Order of Battle reveals that the unit the Scout Platoon and other elements of the 2nd Battalion, 47th Infantry (Mechanized), encountered was a battalion (augmented) of the 88th NVA Regiment. Their regimental battle flag is now framed, and through the generosity of Bill McCaskill, who personally captured it, now hangs in a place of honor in the Regimental Museum maintained by the 2nd Battalion, 47th Infantry, at Fort Benning, Georgia.

For actions in Widows' Village and later in the village of *Ho Nai*, the Scout platoon consisting of 40 Scouts and 2 attached Medics, were awarded three (3) Distinguished Service Crosses, the Nation's second highest award for valor, six (6) Silver Stars, which are the third highest award for bravery, and twenty-two (22) Bronze Star Medals with "V" device, and more than twenty (20) Purple Hearts. My company commander at the time, CPT Jesse Alexander, actually wanted to nominate me for the Medal of Honor, but I told him that I did not think that my actions were at that level to deserve such an award. In retrospect, the actions of SSG Robert Schultz were indeed worthy of the award of the Medal of Honor, and I will forever regret not insisting on his nomination for that most worthy recognition. The Scouts suffered three (3) KIA, four (4) WIA serious enough to be Medevaced Stateside, while other walking wounded remained with the unit. Officially, the Scouts were credited with 77 enemy KIA and 22 POW's; however, a more accurate tally, including actions in the village of Ho Nai, raised this total to 110 KIA and 33 POW's.

Postscript: As with all of the preceding stories, vignettes, tall tales or outright lies, whichever word you choose to call them, there is an abiding element of thanksgiving at their respective endings. When I first wrote this story about "Widows' Village," it was part of a healing process that I was going through with a few other Vietnam Veterans, and this project required some effort on my part. We had been asked by our "team" leader to write about the most traumatic experience that we had encountered or lived through, and the Tet Counter-Offensive was my particularly seminal moment. It was only later, after writing the preceding vignettes that I reminded myself that I had not yet expressed any gratitude or positively acknowledged any people or factors that contributed to my successes from the story.

First and foremost, I would like to thank my Lord and Master for the gift of the "blue veil," to me a very real and personal manifestation of God's power and Grace. Whether it was actually an angel, or the Holy Spirit Himself is a matter of theological debate, the very presence of some Heavenly form of protection cannot be argued, at least not by me. Without that Gift, I would not be able to have penned these words or to do anything else for that matter. I would not have been able to actively participate in the Kairos Prison Ministry, an activity to which I genuinely feel compelled to do, a righteous activity that is my personal calling. And while I'm on the subject of Gratitude, I also want to publicly acknowledge my thanks for God's Ultimate Gift, my salvation which has been bought by such a high price - the sacrifice of His Son, my Lord and Master.

And there certainly is a plethora of earthly mortals that are also deserving my thanks, for without their contributions of loyalty, professionalism, *esprit d 'corps*, and boundless enthusiasm, I would not have been able to accomplish the mission that is the hallmark of the Scout Platoon, 2nd Battalion, 47th Infantry (Mechanized). I am especially grateful to Bill "Mac" McCaskill, Danny "Outlaw" Lawless, Frank "Pancho" McIntosh, Robert "Uncle Five" Brantley, George "Hoss" Ottesen, Junious Hayes, Lee Wilson, Ray Funderburk, Charles Ashton, Robert Schultz, Richard Vielbaum, Charles Kronberg, Richard Mutchler, "Red" Dotson, David Rehfeldt, Richard "Jesus Saves" Smith, Gene "Country" Lammert, Theodore Ryzcek, Frank Guyton, Milton Baty, Lige "Slim" Saint, Robert Porter, Donald Annarella, Alan Mutchler, Jimmy "Baby Huey" Campbell, James "Buddha" Rowe, and Floyd Bobbitt. The gratitude to Robert Schultz, Richard Vielbaum and Chuck Kronberg is expressed to them posthumously, as they were KIA on that fateful day. Some of the aforementioned Scouts - "Slim," "Hoss," and the Mutchler brothers - have already gone on to their Heavenly Reward - or to the Fiddler's Green, in Scout parlance – but they are still remembered today, and every day. My gratitude also extends to those Scouts who helped train my Platoon for the demands of the Tet Counter-Offensive, men like Emmitt "Snuffy" Smith, Richard "Moss" Bartol, SFC "Moon" Mullins, and a host of others whose names are now faded memory. And I would be remiss if I didn't mention the great contribution to the successful operation in Widows' Village that Company B, 4th Battalion, 39th Infantry played that fateful day. Command Sergeant Major (Ret) Orlando Gallardo was a junior NCO that day, and later provided me with some valuable insights into the supporting assault that his company conducted in Widows' Village. If memory has failed me once again, and I neglected to mention any Scout or Honorary Scout, please forgive me and send me a personal letter. And of course, I cannot exclude LTC John E. Tower, aka Panther 6 from this gratitude list, thanking him, at least posthumously as well, for the magnificent example of how a great battalion commander should act. I genuinely tried to emulate his example later on in my military career while serving as the commander, 1st Battalion, 141st Infantry (Mechanized), part of the Texas Army National Guard.

Assorted Poetry and Poetic Tributes

MAKING PROGRESS

And the war progresses,
    With cannons arcing their loads of death,
Choppers ferrying the living, dying and dead,
    With beans and bread, a lovely meal
For the devil, who cares?

A stop in a village
    Unspeaking faces do not disclose friend or foe,
You smile, but they know
    Neither for friendship or leering
At their plight, afraid to go into the fields
    To harvest their rice.
Two brave souls venture forth
    And four more friends come to retrieve
Torn bodies, victims of well-concealed mines.
    Innocent, guilty, all pay for trespassing
Into the world of the enemy.

And cannons boom,
    Choppers slap the air in defiance
Of gravity, or are they making
    Their own plea against insanity?
Another man dies,
    And war progresses,
But does Man?
                May 1968, RVN

[The following was written as a tribute to Ralph Mike Velasco, a Scout who was killed in action in 17 January 1968. Mike was from Los Angeles, California.

TO MIKE

As I carried the stained helmet
Back to the circle of safety,
I noticed that tears
Made a darker, more eternal mark
Than blood.

I mourned the loss
Of one brave man,
But heard Man's eternal dirge.

I had won the battle,
And as I bathed my wounds,
The plaintive cry of Man
Filled my ears with the plea
"Why war? Why me?"

27 January 1968

[The following haikus, a form of poetry adapted from the Japanese, were written exactly twenty years after the Tet Offensive, on January 31, 1988.]

HAIKUS FOR DEPARTED SCOUTS

It has been only
Two hundred forty short months
Since that sanguine day.

And still I am drawn
Like a moth to those events
When you were called Home.

Your deeds of valor
That are not yet committed
To song or to bronze.

CHANGES

It left us all different
    Then we were before,
Strange sounds never heard
    Ever wanting them to go away.

There were new friends made
    Brothers in the dirt and air
They were there for a year
    Some went home sooner.

We came fresh, young and naïve
    Not quite ready for the task
Of sleeping in water, bleeding in woods
Areas not yet ready for us either.

Was it the weight on our shoulders
    Reminiscent of our primordial parents
Carrying the spoils of hunt or war
    That reverted us to caves?

We reveled in unearthly power
    Delivered in ways of air and land
Butchers of flesh and trees
    Yet quietly yearning for home.

[This poem is dedicated to the memory of SSG Robert Schultz, killed in action in the Republic of Vietnam, 31 January 1968, while serving with the Scout Platoon, 2nd Battalion 47th Infantry (Mechanized), 9th Infantry Division, written on the 18th anniversary of his death. As noted elsewhere, SSG Schultz was posthumously awarded the Distinguished Service Cross and the Purple Heart.]

EIGHTEEN YEARS LATER

Have you ever had the chance
    To never say "good-bye"
To someone passing through your life
    Who's not afraid to really try?

Have you ever longed for one more day
    To find the words unspoken
To someone and his martial vows
    Unsullied now, still unbroken.

Have you ever sensed the wonder
    Of the Courage to toss the die
Regardless of the score that shows
    Mindful of the will to try.

Have you ever had the chance
    To never say "good-bye"?
Thank you, Robert Schultz,
    Thank you for passing by.

NEW RAIN

Able to sit outside
In my city forest
Listening to raindrops
And watching the flashes
Of far distant lightening

Without smelling the fear
That lived in the jungle
Where rain chilled and muffled
Where flashes were too close
Or lightening was mortar.

Quiet, nurturing raindrops
Calmly splashing on my
Purely urban sidewalk,
Nearby lightening cleansing
My air so freely breathed.

April 9, 1986

[The following articles are reprints of stories that were printed in the *Austin Statesman* and as the name changed, in the *Austin American-Statesman* during my second tour of duty in Vietnam. I am grateful to the newspaper for originally printing them in 1970, and for the permission to reprint them here.]

Only Uncertainty in the Minds of Vietnam-Bound Soldiers –
March 18, 1970   Story I

"Flight Tango 2 Bravo 3! Now loading for Bien Hoa Air Base. All passengers manifested on this flight report to Gate 2!" Somehow, the announcement had an unreal sound to it, like it was not a conscious moment. But as I sat down in the airline seat and fastened the safety belt, reality slowly crept back in, only to be accelerated by the starting whine of the jet engines.

Soon the airplane streaked its way into the inky night, leaving America behind, but carrying a portion of America with it. Most of the passengers were "first-timers," young men joking, laughing as they boarded the plane, but becoming a bit more somber as the fight began. Questions about the unknown were on every face, a very natural emotion. One can only speculate what was going on in their minds; thoughts of home, "war stories" form veterans, and a gnawing uncertainty of the future.

Boredom, occasionally interspersed with coffee, napping, meals, and small talk was the order of the day. Five hours to Honolulu, another 10 hours to Kadena, on Okinawa where the plane was refueled. In another three hours and 30 minutes, we would touch down, albeit fleetingly, at *Bien Hoa*. Very likely, a group of homeward bound soldiers would be anxiously awaiting not our arrival, per se, but that of the "Big

Freedom Bird." Their year now over no hesitation could be anticipated in boarding the aircraft.

Soon the coastline of Vietnam came into sight, and shortly thereafter, the telltale sound of lowered landing gear made the country all the closer. At 2:32 p.m., Vietnam time, Flight Tango 2 Bravo 3 touched down, signaling the beginning of another year that each person, that is, the ones who would be returning intact, would start marking off on his personal calendar. Ahead lay the uncertainty of unit assignment, job, and the anticipated reunion with loved ones. The year of waiting had begun.

Making Progress – February 2, 1970   Story II

Enroute to my new assignment as company commander of Delta Company, 5th Battalion 12th Infantry, I was immediately impressed by the significant changes in the Vietnamese countryside as compared to my first tour. As we drove along *Quoc Lo* (National Highway) 1, I noticed that all of the houses in the villages of *Ho Nai* and *Long Lac* had recently been wired for electricity. And when we turned onto *Quoc Lo* 20, heading for Fire Support Base Libby, field headquarters of the Battalion to which I was assigned, there was no need for an armed escort.

While electric city power and a relatively secure highway may appear inconsequential and may be taken for granted in American, for a country like Vietnam, improvements such as these do not go unnoticed. The cynic may argue that the installation of electric service in the heavily populated villages along *Quoc Lo* 1 is only "window dressing." This charge may be valid indeed, since *Quoc Lo* 1 is the busiest highway in the Republic. On the other hand, the proximity of generating stations in Saigon, *Long Binh* and *Bien Hoa* would make adjacent villages the logical choice for electric service. Whatever the motive, several thousand more houses were now afforded the relative luxury of electric power, the product of Vietnamese-American cooperation. Interestingly enough, all of the houses, from the well-constructed villas to the mud wall and thatched roof variety were electrified.

During my first tour of duty in Vietnam, *Quoc Lo* 20 had acquired the infamous nickname of "Ambush Alley," because of the frequent Viet Cong attacks on military convoys moving in the area. Occasionally, civilian buses were also ambushed, more often only stopped while the VC extracted their "safe-conduct" taxes. If ARVN –Army of the Republic of Vietnam –soldiers were travelling on that bus in uniform, they were usually taken off, and shot by the roadside. To drive the 21.5 kilometers to the fire support base without armed escort, and more importantly, without incident, was a new experience! In the past, the deteriorated condition of the highway dictated a slower speed, thereby increasing the possibility of a successful enemy ambush or roadblock. But now, thanks to the efforts of the US Army Engineers, *Quoc Lo* 20 is now a high-speed highway. In fact the road is so conducive to faster travelling that our truck drivers have to be reminded to slow down while going through the hamlets and villages. The civilian buses and trucks now travel *Quoc Lo* 20 apparently with less fear of the VC ambushes or roadblocks, bringing people and produce to the markets of *Xuan Loc, Bien Hoa* and other cities. But these people, having lived with a war, off and on for thirty years, know that security can be a fleeting thing.

By providing electric service and improving highways by the RVN government, it can also create a double-edged sword. First of all, the efforts to upgrade utilities will substantiate the government's claim that it is concerned with the welfare of the population. Secondly, if the VC interrupt the power supply or interfere with vehicular traffic by destroying part of the new highway, their claims of 'being a friend of the people' will have an even more hollow ring. The ability of the average Vietnamese to have electric lights in his home and to travel the highways more safely are tangible evidence of progress in this area of Vietnam.

Taking Command – February 20, 1970   Story III

As the chopper circled the small clearing in the jungle, I could see the faces of the men hidden in the nearby wood line. Those are the men, I thought to myself, that I would soon be leading into combat. What would they be like? How would they respond to the icy sound of rifle shots cracking overhead through the trees? At the same time, I could almost read their thoughts: what kind of guy would the "newfer" be like? "Newfer," that I was, I was soon to find out, that the term was the local GI term for a "new fellow." In the next few minutes, our mutual questions would be answered at least partially.

The cloud of swirling dust kicked up by the departing chopper soon settled, and the brief and very informal assumption of command ceremony took place. "Sir, these are your platoon leaders, and over here is the command post group, consisting of your radio operators, medic, and artillery forward observer." Without further ado, for saluting has no place in the jungle, I briefed the platoon leaders on our new mission. We were to find and destroy local Viet Cong forces that were continuing to extort food and taxes from a hamlet several "klicks" to the south. "Klicks" is the abbreviation for 'kilometers', the linear measure for the Army topographic maps.

During the briefing, the resupply chopper arrived with cases of C-rations, water and mail. Resupply causes a variety of emotions, ranging from joy to gripes. Even as unappetizing as C-rations and warm water may sound, to a hungry GI, it's better than nothing at all! On the other hand, there is the countervailing thought of having to carry the additional weight of six meals and five quarts of water that every resupply brings. When the C-rations are opened, there is some active bargaining. "I'll trade you a beefsteak for a turkey loaf." The response was, "OK, but throw in a can of pears, and it's a deal!" More questions, such as "Who's got something to swap for a pecan roll?" and "Know anybody who likes fruit-cake?" Fruit cake – in small cans – appeared in every case of C-rations, and fruit cake in April in the middle of the jungle was a thought that was almost too incongruous to consider.

Walking, or to use the GI vernacular, "humpin'" through the jungle presents some problems as well as some advantages. In this particular are of Vietnam, the jungle has a triple canopy, with a variety of vines growing near the ground. Trying to walk through the jungle while carrying an 85 pound rucksack that seems to snag on every other vine is not the fastest way of travelling. Because of the dense vegetation, it is impossible to see more than 20 inches either direction, a handicap for both the enemy and for us. On the other hand, the jungle offers us some cover from Ol' Charlie, who may have an ambush setup in the cleared areas. And that triple canopy gives some respite from the searing pre-monsoon sun.

By 1630 hours – that's 4:30 pm to the civilian world – we were still far from our objective area, so we started looking for a place to spend the night. Setting up a "night-time" is more than throwing down that cumbersome pack that now seems to weigh 150 pounds! It means accomplishing a multitude of tasks, like setting up the trip flares used for early warning of approaching enemy, emplacing the Claymore anti-person-nel mines, and coordinating the defensive fires between the platoons. While this is being done, my artillery forward ob-server and I are plotting the defensive concentrations – Delta Charlies in code – around our position and in the vicinity of the other platoons. Night locations are radioed to battalion headquarters, and then we wait for the next dawn.

There are other rituals attendant to the end of a day, like

warming a can of C-rations, finding the least insect-infested place to sleep, one that is preferably near a big tree to hide behind, and silently reflecting on home. And then the mosquito repellant, which causes one to break out in a mild sweat, but at least gives some protection from the variety of bugs. The repellant is applied over a face that has not seen either a bar of soap or a razor in the past several days, over a face that is washed by one's own perspiration. But another day is about to be struck off the Big Calendar!

Finally, the first rays of sun begin to creep through our jungle roof. How did the day start at home? Memory recalls a little boy, climbing in bed beside me and saying, "Hi, Daddy!" Back to reality, I fumble for a used C-ration can and begin brewing my morning cup of coffee. By the time all of the powdered coffee and cream have dissolved to their fullest extent, leaving a few floating lumps in the process, my radio operator hands me the decoded message from battalion of today's operation order. In between a few cigarettes, a warmed can of pecan cake roll or some other C-ration delicacy, I start to write the operation order for the other platoons. So begins another hunt for Charlie.

The ambush was well planned. As in all the other ambushes, patience was to be practiced. We set up along a heavily used trail leading from the jungle through the coffee plantation and eventually to the hamlet. And then, movement along the trail, and contact! When the action is over, the captured weapons equipment and documents are gathered and the information is relayed to battalion. Hastily, we leave the ambush site, and walk to the hamlet where the American advisor of the Vietnamese Popular Forces is informed that part of the threat to his hamlet has been eliminated.

The message came from battalion that we were to return to Fire Support Base Libby. The news of a few days' break raced through the company. "Hey, do you think they'll have enough cold beer back there?" "I heard that ol' Sarge scrounged some steaks for a barbecue!" "Whooee, cold beer and steaks!" Soon the US Army trucks rumbled up the road to the hamlet. The ride back was anything bit quiet – a happy bunch of GI's enroute to a well-deserved rest.

An Airmobile Operation in Vietnam –
March 15, 1970   Story IV

Rockets and miniguns fire burst from the gunships accompanying our airmobile operation, and exploded all around our proposed landing zone. The Eagle Flight of Delta Company had begun, as the first lift of six Hueys maneuvered into final formation. As the choppers neared the ground, men began to climb out and stand on the landing skids, hoping to bet a faster start in their dash for the nearby wood line. After the first lift was completed and the wood line secured, I radioed back to the battalion commander in his chopper overhead, "Spacer 28 this in Mike 28' the Lima Zulu is cold!" With this report of a secure, uncontested landing zone, the battalion commander ordered the other two lifts of my company to join us. Delta Company, after a pleasant three days of rest, was returning to the jungle.

On the third day, we found a bomb crater that would serve as our resupply point, and the "Food Bird" was called. Soon, cases of C-rations, water, radio batteries and mail were being tossed out of the chopper, and the resupply ritual began again. In between culling out the unsavory meals and reading a few letters from home, I briefed the platoon leaders on their respective missions: ambush in strategic locations in an attempt to interdict the enemy rocket unit that has been harassing *Long Binh* Post, *Bien Hoa* Air Base and adjacent villages. As the second platoon was moving out to a suspected trail network, there was a terrific explosion followed by machinegun and small-arms fire. The other platoons were immediately deployed to assist the beleaguered element and to set up a blocking position in case the enemy attempted to withdraw. "Mike 28, this is Mike 91. Get some gunships here! They've got us pinned down and are trying to flank us!" I informed Mike 91 that the Cobra gunships had already been alerted. "This is 91, better get a Dust-off too, as we took some hits." All of this information was relayed to the battalion, and soon they responded that Dust-off 36 would be on station in 15 minutes. Before the Dust-off ship arrived, I received a call, "Mike 28, this is Dragon 34, a light fire team and I hear that you have a little work for us." "Roger that, we'll mark our position with smoke! Put the rockets about 50 feet in front of the smoke on a gun-run of west to east – I say again, west to east!" I remembered a very tragic incident from my first tour when the gunships made a gun-run right over some of my troops, a bad tactical decision, resulting in 2 American KIA's and the severe wounding of a friend of mine, Dennis Klingman. The gunships enabled us to break contact long enough to get the Dust-off ship in and the wounded evacuated. Only one of my troops' wounds was serious but I sent in most of the other wounded to receive better medical attention than we could provide in the field. Then we settled down to a cautious watch, waiting to see if Charlie would return. The night passed uneventfully enough.

Since the last contact, we had seen no sign of the enemy, either fresh trails or rocket launching sites. In addition to our search operation, we had the mission of finding a suitable re-supply point for our food and water level was getting low. But it seemed that the harder we looked, the denser the jungle canopy became. Finally after six hours of 'breaking brush,' we found a spot where the supplies could be dropped while the copper hovered above us. This type of resupply is especially dangerous, for not only do we have to guard against Charlie taking pot shots at so inviting a target as a hovering copper, we had to stay out of the way of the falling canisters of water and the boxes of C-rations.

After I had insured that the platoons had formed a secure perimeter around the drop zone, I settled down for a drink of water and a quick smoke before the chopper arrived. My artillery forward observer war already resting, so I joined him and asked if he was ready to shoot some steel if need be. "Roger that, Charlie Oscar – (Charlie Oscar was the phonetic alphabet for 'commanding officer') - by the way, what kind of snake is light green in color and has a thin yellow stripe down the side?" That type of description could only fit one snake that I knew of, the venomous bamboo viper. When I asked why he would ask such a question, he replied, rather unemotionally, "Well, there's one down by your feet!" Repressing a tremendous urge to leap into the air, I called for someone to bring me a machete, in a very quiet voice. I know that snakes don't have ears, but I wasn't giving this Johnny No-Shoulders a chance to hear me. Finally, someone handed me a "prang," the Australian version of the machete, and with a fast swing, there was one less bamboo viper in Vietnam. Not that he would be missed, but what worried us was the whereabouts of his mate! Naturally I was a bit more careful of where I sat down from then on!

The next morning, I found my radio operator frantically trying to decipher an encoded message from battalion. These types of messages are always cause for alarm, since they can be advance warning of suspected enemy attacks, or orders to move an exceptionally great distance. Either case causes a great deal of sweat. But this message proved to be an exception: Move by the most expeditious route to Fire Support Base Gladys. Two days later, after walking through 8500 meters of dense jungle, some of the thickest I had ever encountered, we spotted FSB Gladys on the next hill. "Hey Charlie Oscar, can we bathe in the river?" Before I could answer, a voice shouted back, "Not you, Pig Pen, you'd leave a ring like a bathtub!" FBS Gladys was built about 50 meters away from the *Dong Nai* River, and was a strategic point, guarding against the VC using the river to access attack positions near *Bien Hoa* and other vital Allied posts. And so it was, another completed mission, another bath, albeit in the rather muddy water of the *Dong Nai*, and preparation for the inevitable repetition of more missions later.

Life at a Fire Support Base – April 7, 1970   Story V

Fire Support Base Gladys was one of the two outposts maintained by the 5th Battalion, 12th Infantry. Situated on the *Dong Nai* River that acts as the northern boundary between *Bien Hoa* and *Long Khanh* provinces, this fire base is one of the more remote posts in our area of operation. Almost totally dependent for supplies on the daily Chinook helicopters, there is affair-weather road that leads through the long-abandoned hamlet and rubber plantation of *Thanh Dang*, to a useable road. But with the monsoon season rapidly approaching, and with it, the inevitable deep mud, the road would have to be counted out as a means of resupply.

To the north of FSB Gladys is the *Dong Nai* River, which also formed a barrier between us and War Zone D, clearly visible and ominous in appearance. War Zone D had been the scene of some of the fiercest fighting earlier in the war, and the vegetation still reflected the intensity of the battles. Adding to the desolation was the ubiquitous results of Agent Orange, meaning much bare earth with a total lack of plant growth. Carved out of the jungle, FSB Gladys plays an important role in support in combat operations in both War Zone D and in the War Lord District, immediately to the south and southwest. When Delta Company as arrived at FSB Gladys for a much needed rest, we immediately set about upgrading the defensive posture of the camp. Only a week before, another base had been heavily mortared and then attacked by ground forces. To preclude our being next on Charlie's attack list, we embarked upon an extensive work program. So armed with machetes, demolitions and chain saws, we began to hack away at the jungle surrounding the FSB. Additional concertina wire and trip flares were installed to supplement the existing defensive mechanisms around the perimeter. Through neglect by previous occupants, several of the bunkers on the perimeter appeared to be on the verge of collapse, so our own "urban renewal" program was to be evidenced inside the base itself.

Working in the early morning hours before the heat became unbearable, we began to see some results in less than two weeks. The afternoons were devoted to marksmanship practice and to swimming in the river. But as we all knew, our stay at the "R&R Center on the *Dong Nai*" could not last much longer. On the morning of the fifteenth day, Delta Company walked out of FSB Gladys, but little did we realize that it would be for the last time. When Bravo Company of the battalion moved in to replace us, we hoped that they would be appreciative of the many hours of labor that were spent making FSB Gladys a bit more livable and secure.

Two days, later, battalion called, "Mike 28, this is Spacer 34. Move to the nearest Papa Zulu (pickup zone) for immediate extraction." Since the normal cycle for jungle operations is 14 days at a minimum, everyone guessed that something big was in the planning stages. Naturally, the "Rumor Monster" cranked up his efforts and put the Rumor Mill into high gear. "Hey, I hear we're going to Saigon for Ho Chi Minh's birthday." Since the VC-NVA have a nasty habit of launching attacks on that day and on other significant days, the possibility of our deployment to Saigon was entirely feasible. "Maybe the 199th is going home!" This rumor had persisted from the time that I first joined the Brigade back in February, but so far, it was just another GI rumor. Another voice piped up, saying, "I've got $20 that says we're going to Cambodia!" That voice turned out to be the most prescient one that I heard in months.

As we scrambled for the choppers that were settling down on our PZ, each man would have to answer his own question, at least until more and better information could be found. Soon landing at the Brigade Main Base, word reached us to prepare for operations in Cambodia. With that bit of news, our one question was answered, only to be replaced by many others. And there would be plenty of new questions.

Mission to Cambodia – May 20, 1970   Story VI

[Previous parts of this story were reported in the vignette about the long-armed chopper pilot!]

    ... The Eagle Flight was completed without further incident, and our search of Base Area 351 began. We were soon to discover that Cambodian mosquitoes and leeches are more voracious than their Vietnamese cousins, and that the hills of Cambodia are steeper than those across the border. By the time that the battalion had returned to Vietnam, we had captured 350 tons of rice, over 450 weapons, 500,000 rounds of small-arms ammunition and almost 5,000 rounds of rocket or mortar ammunition. In terms of restricting further enemy activities, this was sufficient rice to feed 2,000 troops for a year, enough weapons to arm at least an enemy battalion, and the equivalent large-caliber ammunition to launch 239 indirect fire attacks. One can only speculate on the number of South Vietnamese and American lives that discovery might have saved.

    My unit, Delta Company, 5th Battalion 12th Infantry, was responsible for capturing more than 2,000 bicycles, 386 SKS carbines, 680 hand grenades, 100 pounds of blasting powder, and numerous land mines. We were also credited with finding almost 700 mortar rounds for the 120mm heavy mortar, and five K-62 radios, a type of communication equipment never before found in either Cambodia or in Vietnam.

    On returning to Vietnam, I became aware of a dichotomy of emotions over the Cambodian venture. If we had succeeded in saving some lives, they were lives of people that we did not know, while the operation had cost us some buddies, "Grunts" that were truly known and loved. There was further tragedy in realizing that for the most part, those

weapons and munitions that we had captured were manu-
factured in Red China, a country that obviously could have
better employed their resources in a more constructive capacity than supporting a war. For that matter, this was has not
been very constructive for our country either, and hopefully,
the Cambodian operation will help bring the peace that has
so long evaded Southeast Asia.

[Years after the Tet Offensive by the combined forces of the Viet Cong and the North Vietnamese Army and the Tet Counter-Offensive, involving the US, ARVN, and other Allied forces, a translation of a monograph from one of the major participants surfaced, and is reprinted below. The style, tone and general organization of this article is thinly-veiled pessimism bordering on a brand of fatalism rarely seen in the Communist world. Truth is only in the pen of the author, and hyperbole seems to be the order of the day! In reality, the claims of the authors are so specious, especially in comparison to empirical data that one has to wonder if this bit of historical revisionism was meant as a face-saving or maybe a life-saving gesture. Initially, my goal was to refute the North Vietnamese' version of some history in which I was personally involved, but decided that the readers of this book could decide for themselves after reading more objective history outside of this book of mine. Suffice it to say for many of us that were involved in the Tet Counter-Offensive, reading "The People's Army" version is entertainment enough.

From the authors' own words, the separate and distinct mention of the southern area of Vietnam as 'Cochin China' only reinforces Western authorities' contention that Vietnam was never viewed as a singularly distinct country. Had this series of battles took place in the Central Highlands area, the locals would have been called 'Annamese' by the Tonkinese, those Northerners who habitually viewed to other sections of what is now Vietnam with total disdain. From early in its history, what was then French Indo-China was actually three separate and disjointed countries, whose only brief periods of commonality were during rebellions against invading forces, be they Chinese, Japanese, or French.

In reading the "History of the 5th Division," those with any academic or military experience in the area will doubtless note the fatalistic tone of this piece, written as if the authors were soon to face execution. Fact of the matter is, we don't know what the ultimate fate of the authors was, but I'm certainly glad not to be in their shoes, or in this case, Ho Chi Minh sandals! Happy Reading, Warriors!]

HISTORY OF THE 5TH DIVISION
(LICH SU SU DOAN 5)
Editorial Supervision: Headquarters and Party Current Affairs Committee of Military Region 7
Authors: Lieutenant Colonel Ho Son Dai (Primary editor, Chapter 5, Conclusion)
Major Nguyen Van Hung (Introduction, Chapters 1, 2, 3, 4, and 6)
Assistance provided by Tran Quang Toai
People's Army Publishing House, Hanoi, 1995

Page 118

CHAPTER TWO
PARTICIPATING IN THE GENERAL OFFENSIVE AND UPRISING ON THE EASTERN APPROACHES TO SAIGON
(1968-1969)

After the American imperialists had spent two dry seasons in unsuccessful attempts to conduct a "strategic counter-offensive" using two pincer tactics, "search and destroy attacks aimed at breaking the back of the Liberation Army" and rural pacification operations, by the end of 1967 American forces had been forced into a passive, reactive posture and were being pulled out and stretched thin in accordance with our strategic plans. The defeats on the battlefields of South Vietnam had placed the American government in a difficult economic, political, and diplomatic situation. On the international arena and even inside the United States opposition to the war of aggression had exploded and was growing, creating significant uncertainty and divisions within the American ruling class.

In late December 1967, however, under pressure from the "hawks" in both houses of Congress and from the industrialist warmongers,

Page 119

President Johnson decided to send 100,000 additional troops and additional weapons to South Vietnam, raising U.S. troop strength there to 480,000 men. He also ordered the U.S. military command in Vietnam (MACV) to put together plans for a third strategic counter-offensive. This counter-offensive was to begin in late December 1967 and last until April 1968. The counter-offensive was to focus primarily on a number of targets in the Eastern Cochin China [Eastern Nam Bo] theater of operations.

In the primary theater, Eastern Cochin China, in early December 1967 two brigades of the 101st Airmobile Division were hurriedly moved in to reinforce the Binh Long-Hon Quang-Dau Tieng sector. U.S. mobile reserve forces and the puppet 5th Division hastily carried out an offensive plan aimed at blocking Eastern Cochin China's main force units in Phuoc Long and along Route 14. These forces then launched a counter-attack to capture our revolutionary base areas in Tay Ninh and Song Be. The objectives of the Americans and their puppets in this third offensive campaign were to draw in Liberation main force units to deal with their attacks in order to enable them to isolate and inflict casualties on our 5th, 7th, and 9th divisions; to attack our revolutionary base areas; to push our forces away from the Saigon-Gia Dinh area; to gradually improve the situation and expand the security perimeter surrounding Saigon; and to enable U.S. and puppet forces to retain the strategic initiative.

On our side, after the great victories won by our side during the 1966-1967 dry season, South Vietnam's Liberation armed forces had made major strides in their command organization and ability to command forces in combat and had gained considerable experience in building a people's war posture to respond to the two American imperialist counter-offensives.

Page 120

Assessing the status of the revolution in South Vietnam at that time, in July 1967 a Plenum of the Party Central Committee stated that, "The enemy's limited war strategy has failed at the most basic level and is currently confused and on the strategic defensive on the battlefields of South Vietnam. This is a tremendous failure for the over-all strategy of the American war of aggression in South Vietnam." The Central Committee Plenum directed all battlefields throughout South Vietnam to conduct a fall-winter campaign to push the enemy back onto the defensive and into further difficulties, to develop new strength and a new offensive posture to provide the South Vietnamese revolution with new opportunities, and to move toward securing a decisive victory.

Implementing the orders from the Party Central Committee, the armed forces of Eastern Cochin China focused on massing, consolidating, and building their forces while simultaneously actively preparing the battlefield for the 1967 Fall-Winter campaign.

From the end of the 1967 rainy season onward, Eastern Cochin China's main force divisions, with support from the great rear area in North Vietnam, received reinforcements of both manpower and weapons. They were built into three full-strength main force divisions, each with three infantry regiments and a number of support battalions (mortar, recoilless rifle, 12.7mm anti-aircraft, engineer, reconnaissance, signal, medical, transportation, and sapper battalions). Their weapons and equipment were upgraded with new weapons and various types of technical equipment to support command and communications from the company up to the division level.

Page 121

After an extended period of arduous combat operations in the remote Ba Ria-Long Khanh area, in late September 1967 5th Regiment and the 5th Division's combat support units marched back to Khe Sanh in Phuoc Long to regroup, rebuild, and prepare for the 1967 Fall-Winter campaign. During this period the division was strengthened by the addition of the 88th Regiment to the division's combat formations.

88th Regiment traced its ancestry back to the Tu Vu Regiment of the 308th Division, which as the first main force unit in the People's Army of Vietnam had fought and scored outstanding combat victories in our nation's resistance war against the French colonialists. In June 1965 the regiment received orders to march south to fight in South Vietnam. In 1967 the regiment moved down from the Central Highlands to join the battle in Eastern Cochin China. In September 1967 88th Regiment became a part of the combat formations of the 5th Division. At this time Comrade Sy was the Regimental Commander and Comrade Ba Lanh was the Regimental Political Commissar.

Upon their return to Khe Sanh to participate in the Fall-Winter campaign, the units of 5th Division vigorously reorganized, held political training classes to digest the content of the Central Committee Resolution, and received

supplementary training to help them built resolve to successfully accomplish their assigned missions during the 1967-1968
Winter-Spring Campaign. During this period the unit made
tremendous efforts. In only a little over one month, 5th
Regiment and the division's support units received and as-
similated 500 new recruits, together with new equipment and
weapons, while at the same time conducting supplementary
training and strengthening the unit's Party chapters at the lowest levels.

Page 122

By early November 1967 the division had reorganized
and strengthened its three infantry regiments (4th, 5th, and
88th Regiments) and its nine support battalions and was hurriedly preparing to launch the campaign. The entire division
participated in political training to build combat resolve.
The Division Headquarters and Party Committee directed a
campaign of wide-ranging political activities within the Party
chapters with the goal of building "three good" Party Chapters
and having all Party and Youth Group members sign up to
become "Hero Killers of Americans" and "Hero Destroyers
of Vehicles." This campaign created a widespread emulation
movement throughout the entire division.

In the Ba Ria-Long Khanh area, 4th Division worked with
local forces to conduct continuous attacks against enemy
positions along Route 15. In late November, on orders from
the COSVN Military Command in preparation for the 1968
Winter-Spring campaign, 4th Regiment's 2nd Battalion was
ordered to conduct supplemental training in urban combat
operations. Regimental Commander Nguyen Nam Hung and
a sapper reconnaissance cell were sent to infiltrate the city
disguised as a group of vehicle mechanics. There they studied
enemy targets in the Newport and Hang Xanh Intersection

areas and made contact with agents of the revolution to develop infiltration routes for later use to move 2nd Battalion into the city to serve as a deep penetration force and attack targets assigned to it in Phase 1 of the 1968 Spring General Offensive and Uprising. After one month of carrying out the Fall-Winter campaign, COSVN main force units and the armed forces of Eastern Cochin China had eliminated large numbers of enemy troops while at the same time completing preparations of all kinds for the 1968 Spring campaign.

Page 123

Our troops, equipment, and weapons were quickly being moved into the areas around Saigon-Gia Dinh, creating springboard positions north, northwest, southwest, and northeast of Saigon.

As soon as they began to carry out their third strategic counter-offensive the Americans and their puppets were heavily attacked in Tay Ninh, on Route 16 in Tan Uyen, and in the Xuan Loc area of Long Khanh. In mid-December, however, after discovering that our pressure in the area surrounding Saigon-Gia Dinh was growing day by day, Westmoreland personally ordered the postponement of the counter-offensive, withdrew U.S. military units on the outer perimeter north of Saigon, and moved in forces from Vung Tau and the Central Highlands to defend the middle perimeter and the outskirts of the city as a precaution against attacks by our forces.

In December 1967 the Party Politburo issued a resolution on the revolutionary opportunity in South Vietnam and directed the launching of a general offensive and general insurrection throughout South Vietnam. To implement this Politburo resolution, the COSVN Military Headquarters and COSVN Military Party Committee issued the "Quang Trung" resolution to provide guidance for a general offensive and general insurrection. The resolution provided concrete guidance to direct the actions of all Liberation armed forces in South Vietnam. To carry out the Party's strategic design and to directly command and guide the general offensive and general insurrection in the focal point sector of the "Tet 1968 Spring Campaign," the COSVN Military Command and Military Party Committee decided to dissolve the Eastern Cochin China Military Region [Military Region 7] and the Saigon-Gia Dinh Military Region.

Page 124

In their place five sub-regions were formed covering the five primary attack sectors into Saigon. Also formed was Sub-Region 6, consisting of the inner city itself, to directly command the sapper, urban commando, and mass popular political struggle forces in the precincts of the inner city.

In the principal offensive sectors leading to the focal-point targets of the general offensive, we would use COSVN's main force divisions and specialty branch units to attack U.S. and puppet army units to tie down U.S. and puppet main force units on the middle perimeter in order to enable a number of main force units to penetrate into the inner city to cooperate with sapper and urban commando forces in attacking and seizing the important key leadership targets and to support the people in uprisings to seize control of the city.

In the area east and northeast of Saigon (Sub-Region 5 and a portion of Sub-Region 4), the primary attack elements would be 5th Division and COSVN's 724th Artillery Regiment. These units, supported by one sapper battalion from Sub-Region 4 and one Bien Hoa City urban commando company, were assigned the missions of attacking and capturing Bien Hoa Airbase, the U.S. 2nd Field Force Headquarters, the puppet 3rd Corps Headquarters, the Thu Duc Officers School, the Thuc

Duc Electrical Power Plant, and the Bien Hoa Prison, and of supporting local armed forces and the popular masses in uprisings to liberate Bien Hoa City. On 14 December 1967 the Bien Hoa Front was formed. Comrade Tran Minh Tam, acting Commander of the 5th Division, was appointed Front Commander (Footnote: In late November 1967 5th Division Commander Comrade Nguyen The Truong was transferred to a new assignment).

Page 125

Comrade Nam Dung, Deputy Division Political Commissar, was appointed Political Commissar of the Bien Hoa Front. Comrade Tran Cong An, Commander of the Bien Hoa Province Military Unit, was appointed Deputy Front Commander, and Comrade Phan Van Trang, Secretary of the Bien Hoa City Party Committee, was appointed Deputy Political Commissar.

To ensure the maintenance of secrecy for the attack while at the same time moving forces down to the targets to be in place on time to open fire when the campaign was launched, on 20 January 1968 the Bien Hoa Front Headquarters sent cadre forward to conduct reconnaissance of the targets while simultaneously ordering the units to begin their approach marches. On the night of 20 January a cadre team assigned to reconnoiter the Bien Hoa Airbase left Trang Bom to close in on the enemy to study U.S. troop deployments around the airbase. The cadre team was made up of Comrades Tran Minh Tam, Tran Cong An, Nguyen Minh Thang, and a sapper-reconnaissance element. After one day and night spent clinging to the enemy positions, the cadre team was both tired and hungry. As they departed the area our reconnaissance team encountered an enemy ambush. The enemy detected our team's presence, opened fire, and surrounded them. The entire cadre team had to dive into an underground culvert next to the Binh Sau strategic hamlet to hide. Hearing the gunfire, local guerrilla teams quickly moved in to block the enemy force. They rescued our study team and provided guides that led the group safely back to the base area.

On 25 January 5th Regiment and the division's combat support units received their orders to participate in the campaign. They were directed to rapidly move their personnel to the designated assembly positions and arrive at the pre-determined time.

Page 126

The units marched day and night, crossing rivers, cutting trails, eating dry rations and drinking cold water in order to arrive in time to open fire on schedule. By the night of 29 January 5th Regiment had crossed the Dong Nai River and arrived at its assembly point at Hamlet 3 of Tan Dinh village. The division's combat support units had arrived at the division's forward command post at Hoc Ong Ta. 4th Regiment (under the command of Deputy Regimental Commander Nguyen Minh Thang and Deputy Regimental Political Commissar Nguyen Minh Quang) marched from the Suoi Quyt base west of Route 2 to the area west of Trang Bom. 2nd Battalion, the deep penetration unit, accompanied by Regimental Commander Nguyen Nam Hung, was in place in Guerrilla Zone 6 of Thu Duc village. Everyone was prepared for the order to launch the attack and annihilate the enemy.

On the night of 31 January all units moved forward to reach their assault positions in accordance with the plan. In 4th Regiment's assault sector, by 2000 hours 1st Battalion and the Sub-Region 4 sapper battalion had reached the airbase perimeter fence. At 2330 hours all troops of the sapper battalion had penetrated three rows of fence and were deployed along the enemy's patrol pathway. 1st Battalion ran into problems getting past the enemy obstacles deployed outside the fence-line. 3rd Battalion missed its target and lost contact with the regimental command post.

In 5th Regiment's sector, 1st and 2nd Battalions had closed on 2nd Field Force Headquarters at 2200 hours. While deploying its forces into attack formation 1st Battalion ran into the enemy headquarters outer perimeter security forces and had to halt in place. Meanwhile 2nd Battalion had reached the perimeter fence around the Field Force Headquarters' helicopter landing field.

Page 127

3rd Battalion and the Bien Hoa sapper company had been given the mission of attacking the puppet 3rd Corps Headquarters. While approaching the target 3rd Battalion ran into an enemy force deployed in an outer blocking position and was forced to deploy into attack formation one kilometer from the objective. In accordance with the coordination plan, the sapper company had moved its troops in and deployed in accordance with the attack plan. At 2250 hours, of the attack formations of 5th Division and Bien Hoa's armed forces, only three battalions, one company, and the artillery units had occupied their assault positions. Three battalions and one sapper company, blocked by enemy forces, had not yet reached their assault positions.

Faced with this difficult situation, the Front Headquarters decided to proceed with the attack at the campaign's scheduled "H" hour. The Headquarters issued orders to 1st Battalion, 4th Regiment that when we began shelling Bien Hoa Airbase the battalion was to quickly eliminate enemy forces on the outer perimeter, cut the wire, and attack alongside the sapper battalion to seize their assigned objectives in the northern portion of the airbase. Headquarters told 3rd Battalion, 5th Regiment that when it heard the sound of gunfire the battalion was to quickly mass its forces to attack the enemy position on the outer perimeter and then attack and capture the puppet 3rd Corps Headquarters. The battalion was then to deploy one company to block enemy counter-attacks along the main road and cut the footpath through the area of the Ho Nai station. 1st Battalion, 5th Regiment, was ordered to overcome all obstacles, push its assault formation forward, and mount an attack in coordination with 2nd Battalion to overrun the assigned targets in the 2nd Field Force Headquarters. 4th Regiment maintained contact with other units and moved 3rd Battalion in to occupy its assigned positions.

Page 128

At 0000 hours on 31 January the Tet 1968 General Offensive and uprising began!

On the Bien Hoa Front, 1st Battalion, 274th Regiment fired three volleys of DKB [122mm] rockets into the enemy command center on the airbase. Other types of heavy weapons fired barrages against enemy petroleum storage tanks, ammunition bunkers, troop barracks, and aircraft hangars and revetments. The soldiers of Sub-Region 5's sapper battalion quickly overran enemy positions along the patrol pathway, and then continued the attack into the airbase. 1st Battalion, 4th Regiment maneuvered to bypass the rubber trees that the enemy had cut down, to climb over the obstacles, lines of spikes and piles of trees, and to cut through the fences to enter the airbase. After 30 minutes of fighting the entire battalion had crossed three fence-lines and joined the sapper battalion in an attack aimed at destroying a U.S. Marine battalion [sic] assigned to reinforce the defenses in the northeastern sector. Our troops fought a ferocious battle against the enemy from

0100 to 0400 hours, our two battalions inflicted heavy casualties on one U.S. battalion.

Even though they had suffered severe losses, supported by enemy tanks and artillery the enemy troops stubbornly launched counter-attacks to block our forces. 1st Battalion and the sapper battalion were unable to penetrate deep into the airbase. At first light, 3rd Battalion, 4th Regiment opened fire in the southeastern sector of the airbase. After four hours of passive reaction to our surprise attack, with most of the enemy pulling back and putting up only weak resistance, at 0500 hours on 1 February the enemy began to launch a series of powerful counter-attacks.

Page 129

Enemy helicopters circled overhead, dropping flares and firing volleys of rockets and streams of 20mm cannon fire into the combat formations of 4th Regiment and the sapper battalion. Enemy infantry and tanks edged forward, pushing our attack spearhead back through the airbase perimeter fences. The situation became extremely difficult for us. The battalions ran out of B-40, B-41, and AT anti-tank ammunition. Our casualties soared to almost 50%. In spite of these problems our units continued to fight back with incredible heroism. At 0530 hours enemy aircraft bombed and napalmed 4th Regiment's command post. The regiment was ordered to pull back to the division's forward command post.

At 0700 hours in the morning one enemy battalion and two troops of armored vehicles surrounded 1st Battalion and the sapper battalion on three sides. Savage fighting broke out on the northeastern perimeter of the airbase. 1st Battalion, supported by the sapper battalion, drove back one of the enemy's tank and infantry columns and managed to move its units to the outside. At 1100 hours, when 4th Regiment reached the division forward command post at the "Motorcycle Base," the Americans, using armored personnel carriers, closed in on the regiment by following field telephone lines which we had not had time to retrieve. 4th Regiment established defensive positions that drove back many enemy counterattacks, destroying five M-113s and killing many enemy troops.

In 5th Regiment's sector, in the area of 1st and 2nd Battalion's planned attack on 2nd Field Force Headquarters, at 0115 hours 2nd Battalion opened fire and destroyed the enemy force guarding the airfield. After 30 minutes of fighting, 6th Company drove through a penetration in the perimeter fence to destroy five enemy helicopters.

Page 130

Terrified, the enemy defenders pulled back and used bunkers and pre-fabricated blockhouses to put up a ferocious resistance. At 0400 hours the enemy sent in reinforcements, one Marine battalion and one armored troop. These reinforcements launched a massed counterattack against 2nd Battalion, supported by armed helicopters that laid down heavy fire on the combat formations of 7th and 8th Companies. On the morning of 1 February the enemy sent out troops who tightly encircled 6th Company, which had penetrated deep into the interior of the airfield.

There were also problems in 1st Battalion's attack sector. Our forces were blocked by one enemy Ranger battalion and enemy tanks, which launched a determined counterattack. By 0500 hours the battalion still had not reached its assigned objective. In 3rd Battalion's sector, between 0100 and 0400 hours there was savage close-quarter fighting between our troops and the enemy. At 0500 hours the enemy sent in a battalion of reinforcements that, supported by tanks, attacked 3rd Battalion. Regimental headquarters lost contact with the battalion. The attack columns of 5th Regiment's three battalions all were having severe problems and losses were heavy. Faced with this situation, the Front Headquarters ordered 5th Regiment to pull back to the assembly point.

After receiving these orders, reconnaissance cells were sent out twice to pass orders to 3rd Battalion and 6th Company, 2nd Battalion to break through the enemy lines, but both times all members of the reconnaissance cells were killed. On the third try the reconnaissance troops broke through the enemy line and delivered the orders to 3rd Battalion and 6th Company just as the Americans had encircled them on three sides. Surrounded by enemy troops, 6th Company and 3rd Battalion fought with extraordinary heroism, using every tree-trunk, every mound of earth, every house and fortification to drive back wave after wave of attacks by enemy tanks and infantry.

Page 131

At 1100 hours 6th Company had only about a dozen combatants left, and almost all of these fighters were wounded. Under the command of Deputy Company Commander Nguyen Van Chanh, the company continued to fight on. At 1700 hours the company had only four combatants left, all wounded. Deputy Company Commander Chanh crawled into a drainage culvert to try to find a way through enemy lines. By 1900 hours the last four combatants had all been killed. Although he had multiple wounds all over his body, Deputy Company Commander Nguyen Van Chanh still struggled to escape through the enemy lines. After a night spent stumbling and crawling forward, he had covered more than 10 kilometers and reached the outskirts of the Cay Kho strategic hamlet. On the morning of 2 February Mother Muoi, a local resident, was out looking at her crops when she saw him laying [sic] unconscious on the side of a rice-field dike. She immediately took him home, tended his wounds, and made contact with our agents, who sent him to the division's forward surgical station.

3rd Battalion had been unable to contact regimental headquarters since the morning of 1 January [sic - should read 1 February]. Surrounded by dozens of tanks and two battalions of American troops, the cadre and enlisted men of 3rd Battalion stubbornly dug in and repelled wave after wave of enemy counterattacks. In the area of the Tam Hiep Intersection 12th Company and a recoilless rifle element from 22nd Battalion drove back a series of counterattacks by two Marine companies and dozens of tanks. At 1500 we still had all traffic on Route 1 cut. The enemy assembled a huge composite force, made up of aircraft, artillery, tanks, and infantry, which concentrated heavy fire to destroy our blocking position at Tam Hiep. Fighting amidst blinding smoke, the 92nd Recoilless Rifle Company, led by Comrade Vo Van Tang, drove back seven counterattacks by enemy tanks and infantry. At 1600 hours, out of ammunition and with his guns smashed, Vo Van Tang, with ten separate wounds all over his body, struggled to support a fellow soldier with a broken leg as he led his unit in an escape through enemy lines.

Page 132

At 1700 hours 3rd Battalion withdrew from the battlefield. During its withdrawal the enemy continued to attack the battalion with artillery and air strikes, inflicting heavy losses on 3rd Battalion.

Meanwhile 2nd Battalion/4th Regiment, the deep penetration force under the command of Battalion Commander Comrade Tu On, attacked the Thu Duc Officers School, supported by Sub-Region 4 forces and Thu Duc self-defense guerrilla fighters. Because we were so heavily outnumbered and because of poor coordination between our own forces, the enemy was able to concentrate his attacks on 2nd Battalion. Our forces made a fighting withdrawal to Guerrilla Zone 6 of Thu Duc village. The enemy encircled the battalion, cutting off all escape routes. 2nd Battalion continued to fight on against the enemy counterattacks. Front Headquarters subsequently transferred the battalion to Sub-Region 4, where it continued to operate in the Thu Duc area.

After two days of determined fighting against vastly superior numbers of American and puppet troops, who had the maximum air and artillery support, even though they had not been able to totally annihilate the enemy or gain complete control of their objectives, the division's units had inflicted heavy losses on enemy forces. They killed hundreds of enemy troops, destroyed 49 enemy tanks and armored vehicles and five aircraft, blew up two enemy ammunition warehouses, and destroyed large quantities of enemy military equipment. At the same time, they had supported the armed forces of Sub-Region 5 and the people of Bien Hoa province in coordinated and simultaneous attacks against important U.S. and puppet targets, inflicting heavy losses and totally upsetting their strategic posture on the battlefield.

Page 133

After withdrawing, however, the division suffered heavy losses of personnel, weapons, and equipment. The number of troops killed, wounded, and missing in two days of combat rose to 728 men. During 5th Regiment's return to base the troops ran out of rice, food, and dry rations as they fought a continuous series of battles against U.S. troops making leap-frog attacks and sweeps into the rear base. Regimental Commander Xuan Thanh was killed during these battles.

The first days of the 1968 General Offensive and uprising were very challenging days for the division. While enduring countless difficulties and adversities, the division also received the whole-hearted support and assistance of all Party and governmental elements and of the people of Bien Hoa. For two straight days the women working in the Sub-Region's civilian coolie labor force braved enemy bombs and shells to transport weapons to the front, to bring hundreds of wounded troops to the rear, and to supply rice, Tet cakes, and drinking water to the troops. Comrade Phan Van Trang, Secretary of the City Party Committee, and the other city leadership cadre remained behind with our rearguard elements to arrange the safe transport of more than 1,000 wounded soldiers from the Bau Tien Surgical Aid Station across the Dong Nai River to the rear.

By 5 February all of 5th Regiment had crossed to the eastern side of the Dong Nai to regroup, reorganize, and receive replacements personnel, weapons, and equipment. Rear Services Group 84 sent porters carrying almost 200 tons of food, weapons, equipment, and supplies to the forward supply warehouse at Bau Ham-Cay Gao for issue to units of the division.

Page 134

With tremendous assistance and support from the local government, the local population, and other friendly units, 4th Regiment quickly regrouped and returned to combat operations. 5th Regiment, on the other hand, continued to regroup and re-equip in preparation for a new mission.

On the eastern approaches to Saigon 4th Regiment and Bien Hoa local forces continuously attacked enemy troop concentrations in the field in the area of Trang Bom and the Long Binh logistics facility. On the night of 18 February 4th

Regiment attacked an American mechanized infantry position two kilometers north of Trang Bom. After two hours of fighting 3rd Battalion and two companies from 1st Battalion had eliminated over 100 enemy from the battlefield and destroyed 70 military vehicles. During that same night of 18 February 2nd Company, 1st Battalion, in cooperation with a recoilless rifle company from 724th Artillery Regiment and a company of Bien Hoa local forces, shelled the Long Binh logistics base, setting two ammunition warehouses on fire and annihilating one company of enemy troops.

4th Regiment's clear-cut victories helped to build combat resolve throughout the Bien Hoa Front and encouraged the division's other units and local armed forces to continue to build on these victories by continuously combating enemy counter-attacks, fighting off enemy sweeps, and conducting ambushes to erode enemy troop strength on the Bien Hoa-Long Thanh perimeter. These attacks inflicted heavy losses on enemy forces.

By the end of Phase 1 of the General Offensive (from 31 January to 15 March 1968) the division's units had eliminated thousands of enemy troops and destroyed 119 enemy vehicles, five aircraft, two ammunition warehouses, and large quantities of equipment and supplies.

Page 135

In recognition of these efforts and achievements, 3rd Battalion, 4th Regiment was awarded the Military Achievement Medal, Third Class. Comrades Nguyen Van Chanh and Vo Van Tang were awarded the Liberation Combat Achievement Medal, Second Class.

CPSIA information can be obtained
at www.ICGtesting.com
Printed in the USA
BVOW03s1549231017

498396BV00001B/56/P